Scream For Me, Africa!

Scream For Me, Africa!

Heavy Metal Identities in Post-Colonial Africa

Edward Banchs

Bristol, UK / Chicago, USA

First published in the UK in 2022 by
Intellect, The Mill, Parnall Road, Fishponds, Bristol, BS16 3JG, UK

First published in the USA in 2022 by
Intellect, The University of Chicago Press, 1427 E. 60th Street,
Chicago, IL 60637, USA

A catalogue record for this book is available from
the British Library.

Copy editor: MPS Limited
Cover designer: Aleksandra Szumlas
Cover (front) and frontispiece image: *Trooper* from Frank Marshall's 2011
Visions of Renegades series. Photo by Frank Marshall.
Cover (back) image: Photo by Lee-Roy Jason.
Production manager: Sophia Munyengeterwa
Typesetter: MPS Limited

Hardback ISBN 978-1-78938-521-2
Paperback ISBN 978-1-78938-859-6
ePDF ISBN 978-1-78938-522-9
ePUB ISBN 978-1-78938-523-6

Part of the Advances in Metal Music and Culture series
ISSN 2752-4426 / Online ISSN 2752-4434

To find out about all our publications, please visit our website.
There you can subscribe to our e-newsletter, browse or download our current
catalogue and buy any titles that are in print.

www.intellectbooks.com

This is a peer-reviewed publication.

Contents

Acknowledgements

Writing a book is a test of patience. How you can manage the time to get the research and writing in, versus the balance in your everyday life can push one to limits that few other challenges can. But, I have loved doing this and my patience has remained within reasonable limits because of the people that have encouraged me and pushed me along when I needed it most.

This book begins and ends with Africa. So much from this continent has fascinated me throughout my adult life and I can only hope to continue fulfilling my insatiable curiosities in the future. To those in Africa who were kind enough to answer the questions I had when composing this book: Thank you! And, to my family who never thought my interests in Africa were crazy, and encouraged me to push forward with my goals, I love you and will forever be grateful for the fact that you are always behind me.

In Togo, my sincerest gratitude to Rock, your brothers, your bandmates and your family for welcoming me into your lives for the brief time I was there. It is not usual to have a foreigner following you around with a notebook, voice recorder and camera, but your hospitality and patience will never be forgotten. Beatrice, thank you so much for your translation assistance and for the incredible meal you and your family provided me.

Kankan, I promised that I would keep your character alive and well in the pages of this book, but your patience during COVID and your insight into your beloved Ghana is definitely not an act. Thank you so much for your wisdom and time. I am very much looking forward to seeing your Ghana with you.

In Kenya, this book's chapter would have been difficult without Rico and Patricia. Your hospitality, your patience and your assistance went beyond anything I could have ever imagined. I cannot thank you enough for showing me a Nairobi I have never seen before and for much needed late-night conversations over our favourite records. To Brian Saibore, Daniel Mwangi, Xenostate, DJ Switch, Talal Cockar, Gun (Straight Line Connection), the members of Powerslide, Crystal Axis and I Am Revenge, thank you all for taking the time to meet with me and for understanding the scope of my project. My apologies to Rash for cutting the interview

I did with your incredible vocalist – pronounced 'Roy'. And to Christian Bass, I could not have asked for a better Nairobi 'roommate' during my visit. More so, I could have never asked for a better friend throughout this. Thank you for your patience with my obsessive, late-night reading and writing while you were trying to sleep in the next room. Sorry if I kept you up.

To Dumi, David Israel, Juice and Vulture in Botswana, thank you. I know I keep saying I need to return to Botswana, but after 2020, I miss your country's tranquility more than ever.

And, to Marq Vas, Gary Walker, Clive Pearson, Dean Smith, Robert 'Stretch' Schoonraad, Claire Martens, Natalie Cowling, David Oosthuizen, Sashquita Northey and Robyn Ferguson: I cannot thank you again for taking the time to speak with me. I know it was a difficult year, but 2020 was the year of Skype for us all. It meant a lot that you would take the time to speak with me, even though you got me out of bed pretty early.

Because few things can actually prepare you for writing a book, it is important to have the comfort of personal and professional guidance to push you along. A rather sizable list is due, and I will do my best in acknowledging everyone I need to in person at some time, but first I need to acknowledge Stacey Marie for somehow – and rather patiently – riding through the vicissitudes of my emotions while conducting the research and throughout my incessant bouts of late-night writing. To Didier Goosens, Nelson Varas-Díaz, Craig Halliday and Claire McGee for your input and for guiding me along to ensure that I never drifted too far off course.

It is fairly bittersweet to have to say goodbye to a few friends during the course of writing this, especially when Herman Le Roux would have thought writing a second book on metal in Africa was super cool. I will miss you, Herman. And to Alex Gordon, I cannot stress how much you will be missed. You are a great friend and an incredible editor. You taught me to dig a little deeper with my questions and to ensure that every reader is considered when writing. It is sad to reach the end of the process knowing you wanted to copy-edit this book and give it a read for me. Knowing that you could not do so was as difficult for me as it was for anyone at the Pittsburgh City Paper who had to pass their stories on to you. Mostly, besides that red pen of yours, we really miss your humour. You and Herman were two of the funniest people I had ever met. Rest well you two.

For the staff at the Gumberg Library at Duquesne University and the Carnegie Library in Pittsburgh, an immense amount of gratitude for your never-ending help and support. To Dylan Lowy for helping me find the way towards Intellect. You helped me more than you would ever know (the Dodgers did get that World Series win after all!). Special thanks to everyone at Intellect for your help in putting this book together.

Introduction

Redefining the Boundaries of Scenes

No two art scenes are alike.

Whether one is discussing heavy metal scenes, rock music scenes, jazz, blues, hip-hop, ballet, theatre and even literary scenes, no two exist as mirror images of each other for any variety of reasons. Every single imagination is shaped by not only desire but also by the circumstances that envelop them; social, political and economical models have directed the manner in which an imagination is able to work, compose, perform and create.

Creative minds – and those who appreciate their results – have long celebrated scenes and their geographic origins, comparing their creative output to those with similar interests in other places. Whether it means looking at towns and cities within their own regions or states, or the work of others in disparate countries and continents, where artists are working from provides an opportunity for the artists to relay these circumstances. Yet, so much of the entertainment that is consumed around the world has a Western origin. Further, Africa and African creativity has continually found itself misunderstood, stereotyped, patronized, overlooked or ignored entirely.

Heavy metal is no different.

This genre, one that has grown to become embraced by fans all over the world, has long been dominated by acts with Western origins, relaying Western struggles. With roots in the British midlands in 1970, heavy metal has grown to encompass different musical perspectives, having splintered into countless sub-genres. Musicians and fans have labouriously honed their dedication into creating scenes that exist within the confines of their locality, which have begun to become better integrated into global markets over time. However, there remain metal scenes that often get overlooked (see also Varas-Díaz 2021; Banchs 2016b; Wallach et al. 2011).

This book is about those various scenes in Africa that seldom get discussed. African metal and rock scenes are often overlooked because they are a disruption of the norm, a disruption of what we have come to expect from Africa and from rock and metal music. Further, Westerners have seldom considered the impact these types of music can have on fans outside of this periphery.

1

My interest in heavy metal stretches back to grade school, when my obsession with the sounds of amplified guitars and the energy that came from listening to heavy metal records grew insatiable. Growing up in rural Pennsylvania, I was unaware of bands existing in my hometown. I figured that the existence of metal bands must have occurred in faraway places such as Los Angeles or New York. That was where bands came from. It seemed impossible for bands to exist where I was living.

It would come as a surprise when I discovered that there were metal bands in my hometown. In fact there were several, performing various styles of rock and metal and existing with varying degrees of ambitions. It felt like stepping into a new world. Embracing the local scene allowed me to discover the punk, hard rock, hardcore and extreme heavy metal that was being performed in our town as well as to connect with those who also shared similar interests. This scene – our scene – existed to not only fulfil our need to bring this music closer to us but to also serve as a communal bond. The latter of which was fulfilled through live spaces. We occupied various spaces throughout town in order to organize performances from local bands, which included abandoned warehouse spaces, a community YWCA, local fire halls and VFW halls (that is Veterans of Foreign Wars, for those who grew up outside of Appalachia!).

Our scene, in a sense, was the gathering of those of us who had something in common, and whether we came together as performers or fans, our shared preference for this style of music (Cohen 1999: 239), its history and its culture guided us. Our scene was defined by us, as participants, our bands and their creative output, our scene's history and origins, and our identity as a scene: one that was rooted geographically in our region, state, country and continent. We knew that ours had its defining characteristics, which Sara Cohen says is intrinsic to any scene as every local scene would have its own 'distinctive characteristics, conventions, and identities' (Cohen 1999: 242). Will Straw defines the way in which scenes are created as heterogeneous 'coalitions' and 'alliances' (cited in Cohen 1999: 245), marked by the musical preferences of individual participants. Likely in bigger cities, too, scenes are clearly marked and defined, leaving room for fungible participation.

Scenes like the one I grew up in, and the ones I would come to embrace as I moved away, exist everywhere because of the willingness of participants to bring heavy metal to life with their own local interpretations, including within the African continent.

What I hope to do in the proceeding pages is to challenge the conversation and assumptions that metal fans may have about local scenes because their scenes act as a representation of who they are, and how they are able to reflect the locale that their scene is based in. Thus, not all scenes are created equally, and not all scenes are able to confront their challenges equally. Whether it is Western perceptions about those who live in non-Western settings, or internal distractions, African metal and rock scenes face difficulties that are unlike any that Westerners would ever imagine.

Africa is a continent that has long been marginalized and generalized. What Westerners know about Africa likely comes by way of assumptions and detrimental stereotypes that glaze over the continent's humanity and contributions. I chose to write this book in order to outline various issues that I felt needed to be discussed in relation to the perceptions and assumptions that outsiders have towards the African continent. *Scream For Me, Africa!* is a collection of chapters that discuss a few of the underlying themes I have noted since I began to research rock and heavy metal music and its culture in the African continent. I have chosen to separate this book into two distinct parts. Part I details how Africa's metal and rock cultures are perceived, looking at metal and rock in Togo, Ghana and Botswana. Part II of this book discusses how two metal scenes, South Africa and Kenya, were able to navigate their way through difficult periods of authoritarianism and political turmoil, and how this is shaping the identity of the musicians in these countries today.

While my original idea was to piece together a work that discussed the growing relationship between decolonialism and heavy metal in Africa, reality, however, forced me to shift my approach because African countries were not created and do not exist equally. Each country (and region) confronts its own set of economic, social and political circumstances. Musicians, therefore, are holding different mirrors up – reflecting the circumstances that only they know how to confront. Thus, this book is presented as a book relating to different issues in different nations.

My approach here was not purely academic. My purpose was to allow the musicians to tell their stories, about their surroundings, their lives and their music. What are their lived experiences like? How is it different from that of Western performers? How do they approach songwriting? Why is this type of music important to them? These were the sorts of questions I asked performers, knowing that the answers were going to vary. What I did not expect, however, was for the answers to be incredibly wide-ranging, thus necessitating a readjustment of my original vision for the book. And most of this was due to where the musicians were from and their interactions within their local scene.

Ethno-journalism explained

Delving into the research that informed this book stemmed from years of studying various African metal scenes by way of immersion and personal communications. I have documented how some metal scenes in Africa had come to fruition while anecdotally detailing the circumstances and challenges faced by the musicians in these countries in another book called *Heavy Metal Africa: Life, Passion and Heavy Metal in the Forgotten Continent* (Banchs 2016b), a book that, while it was not peer-reviewed as it was intended for a non-academic audience, was informed by academic proclivities. This is a style that I refer to as ethno-journalism.

This term reflects my tendency to write about matters with an eye towards a larger audience, one that may not have the academic training to read a monograph, yet still introduces new concepts and ideas that are widely discussed in academia, without dense jargon.

The choice to write a book based on fieldwork stemmed from two reasons. First, I wanted to fulfil a curiosity, to answer the questions I had about heavy metal music scenes throughout the African continent. Second, I had to. There was no academic research that had been published on the subject, and it seemed appropriate to jump in headfirst. Instead of waiting for someone else, I simply began travelling to Africa in order to answer the questions myself. I framed *Heavy Metal Africa* as a travel narrative to engage readers with a first-hand perspective on Africa that could potentially place the reader alongside personal connections, while still maintaining a discourse on the issues at hand as told through the eyes of the musicians I profiled in the book. It was after the publication of the book, and my interactions with academia, that I realized the amount of work I could continue to build on as a result of my entry into Africa's various metal scenes. It became abundantly clear to me shortly after the publication of *Heavy Metal Africa* that my book was incomplete. I had a lot more questions than I did before and challenged myself in the manner I set about accomplishing this.

For me, fieldwork was vital as it was the only way to bridge the necessary requirements needed to fully comprehend the circumstances of what the musicians were faced with and forced to overcome. As noted by George Marcus, while immersive research provides stimulation and ideas, traditional fieldwork 'is focused on observations and understandings emanating from intensive work with informants and access to their situated practices and ways of thinking' (2006: 115). In my own way, academic fieldwork and journalism met halfway, as most reporters are in the middle of the story, gathering as much information as possible. Ethno-journalism enables me to keep my work 'small', to avoid the pitfalls of ethnographers who tend to present their work in enlarged, exaggerated language on paper in order to exude authority and experience (Desmond 2016: 334).

However, and this must be noted, I do not work under the aegis of an applied academic practice. I actively observed and participated in minor instances, such as assisting with the loading and unloading of gear into and out of venues and even working a band's merchandise table for them. Further, when conversing with musicians, I, as a fan, would personally introduce musicians to artists that I enjoy because they were curious as to what motivated me. This experience assisted them as it enabled me to share my preferred bands, some of whom are unknown to residents of nations where only well-known acts such as Metallica, Slipknot, Megadeth and Linkin Park, for example, are the metal and rock acts that the musicians are most familiar with. This scene-crossing also enabled me to gain a relative amount of trust with the participants, which better provided me with a 'you are one of us' (Varas-Díaz et al. 2016: 279) insight into the local scene. Notably, this approach also allowed me to strip away any inclination to exoticize my subjects.

My process involves me personally staying with participants in a manner that allowed for a better observation of their interactions with their circumstances. This is a mutual understanding between the scene participants and myself, which are mutually agreed on. I do not pay for interviews, only offering up the opportunity to provide my own provisions as wages earned by residents of the countries I visit offer a stark reality in income disparity between Africa and the West. As documented in the book, my travels revolve around festivals and concerts, which have allowed me to be present during bands' rehearsals as well as their performances.

Where my method is flawed is in the manner in which I ask questions. Adhering to a more journalistic standard of digging deeper (think of a long-form profile in a magazine or newspaper) into their work ethic, drive and the challenges that they are forced to confront within their countries, questions that would fulfil academic methodology are generally omitted as academic models tend to not be misunderstood by those who have no experience or training within academia. Further, I have not spent years of research in academic settings much like a professional ethnographer would have focusing on one particular region or culture and immersing myself in a foreign language, therefore my knowledge on the country and circumstances is generally approached in the months leading up to my trips via journalistic research, not academic research. Everything I ask musicians is about them, their work and their country based on the circumstances I am witnessing and experiencing myself, and only complement my work with academic research after I have begun to outline my chapters.

If a topic came up in informal conversations, that in retrospect seemed relevant to my research, I would then recontact that individual to clarify what was spoken and request permission to cite their comments. I must note, that for the purpose of this text, none of the quotes cited in this book, except for one, were acquired this way. All of the quotes from musicians in the book were acquired through interviews with the musicians that were conducted at their discretion and with the full knowledge that they were being recorded for the purposes of being cited in this work. When necessary, I would contact musicians again through social media messengers or email to clarify spellings of geographical locations, individuals' names, or for re-confirmation of specific events and details. Follow-up interviews are also cited accordingly.

Given that 2020 was not a conventional year, it must also be noted that the COVID-19 pandemic hampered my travel plans that were being accommodated for the purposes of researching this book. Thus, some of the interviews for this text were done via e-mail or Skype, and are cited accordingly.

Though I must concede that my first book would have strongly benefited from the guidance of academic eyes throughout the editing process, the book you hold in your hand is a better reflection of the academic pursuits that have interested me in the years since the publication of my first book. *Scream for Me Africa!* is not only a continuation of what I set out to do in 2016 but also a reflection of the knowledge I have acquired by way of the academic world, which has allowed me to follow up on the items discussed with musicians and the observations I have had.

Having already familiarized myself with certain African metal scenes and participants, I was able to build on this existing knowledge and push dialogues into research that I felt was missing from the academic world. My thinking has been shaped immensely by the acceptance my research was given in academic circles. The benefit of not writing a book with an intended academic audience allowed me to see what was missing from my work and what else I could do with the knowledge being acquired. However, publishing a book initially without the rigour of a peer-review helped me greatly, notably by providing the metal world with a conversation that it needed to have about the places and themes being researched. Thus, the need to complement my work with academic support.

Metal fans are growing ever-aware of the fact that metal is now a part of the African continent, and whether or not it was previously known to metal fans before, metal has long been part of the continent. Yet Africa's metal contributions are seldom viewed equally, and a lot of this has to do with the manner in which Africans are viewed and heard.

The first chapter of this book digs right into this topic with a discussion about hybridity and the expectations placed on acts from the Global South (a term I will use interchangeably to describe the non-Western world). My research for this chapter took me to the West African nation of Togo where I was able to spend time with the band Arka'n Asrafokor, a heavy metal band that has fully incorporated the music of their Ewe culture. Their sound signifies a turning point in African metal, as many are quick to dismiss their locality in order to honour their heavy metal heroes. Without shedding their influences, Arka'n Asrafokor has chosen to also honour their ancestors and their sacrifices. And, in doing so, they have begun to reinvent Togolese music and expectations.

Life as a metal fan from the West has informed me of metal fans' attitudes towards acts from the non-traditional centres of performance, and the expectations to mark their territory through the hybridity of their locality, thus compromising their existence for the exotictization of their identity. What I hope to do with this chapter is highlight that bands can indeed reflect their home if they choose to without falling into the trap of Western assumptions.

The second chapter of this book highlights the masked band Dark Suburb, an alternative rock band from Accra, Ghana. Choosing to present themselves as skeletons named after figures of Africa's rich history, the masked sextet has used their music to speak for the voiceless in their hometown by spotlighting those who occupy the poorest, often ignored corners of the world – the slums. By advocating for Accra-area slum dwellers, Dark Suburb is challenging perceptions and possibilities within their nation. Unlike the previous chapter, Dark Suburb are purposely using the stereotypical Africa as a way of invoking change.

The third chapter of this book delves into a topic that I have long wished to discuss: 'othering' and the heavy metal scene in Botswana. I chose to begin with the metal scene in this underpopulated, landlocked nation because something happened to African metal when viewers confronted the photographs of Botswana metal fans. The powerful imagery – which made their debut in a *Vice* magazine article (Kahn-Harris 2011a) – was an eye-opener to the Westerners peering at their former colonial subjects. These images reflected something that Africans were never 'supposed' to do: embrace a powerful form of Western art. Westerners had created powerful economic and financial systems that were 'advanced' (to borrow a colloquial expression) because of the overarching and expansionist mechanism – colonialism – that fuelled their capitalist ambitions. Modern Africa was to do no such thing: they were supposed to lay down and watch the world grow around them while the continent collectively kneeled to the world with their heads bowed and a bowl-clutching hand raised.

Much of the dialogue around heavy metal in Africa was formulated around the images from Botswana of leather-clad, Cannibal Corpse T-shirt wearing metal fans, was that expectations set were not expectations met. Africans had found a strong voice for themselves in heavy metal. As Wendt argues, it is art that allows the colonial subject to break away from the bindings of colonialism as self-expression 'bolsters [...] self-respect' (1976: 53) and sheds the caricatures that were created by the colonizers, perhaps too leading to a new form of 'racial intolerance' (1976: 53). And for some Africans, heavy metal is this equalizer. Now, whether metal fans are listening to Slipknot in Uganda, headbanging to Gojira records in Togo, trading Iron Maiden T-shirts in Botswana, debating their favourite Metallica albums in South Africa or screaming along to Megadeth songs in Madagascar, heavy metal has found another home in

Africa. Another place to dig its horns into, and another continent where fans are discovering what they can become through this genre: a new identity, a new culture, one that is without borders, religions, language or colonial baggage. This is not a genre that patronizes, this is a genre that empowers. This is one that just wants the listener to scream along!

The downside of the images of Botswana's metal fans came in the manner in which these photographs were viewed. Batswana metal fans were being 'othered', viewed only as a novelty, less so with the same reverence of their Western counterparts. The othering of the metal fans in Botswana has led to a stereotyping of sorts that has, in my view, only diminished the contributions of the local metal scene, which features international touring acts.

In this chapter, I look deeper at the manner in which the fans of the country are presented by discussing photographs that have been published by at least nine other photographers in a variety of publications, including major media outlets. The effects, in my view, were not positive, but simultaneously these images enabled the Botswana scene to expand beyond its borders.

Part II of this book shifts the dialogue, focusing on two countries, South Africa and Kenya. Both of these nations are two of the more recognizable nations within the continent for a variety of reasons, whether it is success in international sporting events, their celebrities or their popularity among Western holiday seekers. However, for metalheads, the struggle to achieve validation for their scenes has been incredibly arduous. These two chapters will delve more into the political aspect of these two African metal scenes.

Both South Africa's and Kenya's rock and metal scenes are bound by their formation through a history of authoritarianism, with the latter country having a longer, more arduous climb, existing not only under a more perfervid police state but also one enforcing an official policy of racism. And both metal scenes are bound by a youth chasing an identity of their own in order to escape the ills of their post-colonial life: the former was desperate to create a new identity away from the validation to their authoritarian, racist political institution, the Dutch Reformed Church, while the latter was attempting to step away from the cultural ethnicity inscribed into their lives.

For South Africans, music served an important role during a tumultuous political period. While the similarities between these two nations' authoritarianism are found in over-reaching policing desperate to silence those who stood to rout the status quo, the South African police state was ruled by the nation's White minority through a policy known as apartheid.

This chapter will also focus on the only rock and heavy metal scene in the African continent that is comprised mostly White participants. As a result of the scene's primary racial makeup, and considering the nation's political history of apartheid, I consider how this form of music promulgated racial identity from the very beginning, and how the scene of today has used this music to create an identity of their own despite this past and a lingering conservatism that remains omnipresent in South African life.

Kenya's metal scene is one that hobbled through political difficulties to reach its status today. By no means is the nation's rock and metal scene a major focal point for international audiences like the South African and Botswana scenes, yet it has come along well since the nation's transition to liberal democratic elections. Yet there have been substantial hiccups in the decades since, including horrific episodes of violence that have been directly tied to subsequent elections – elections that have forced Kenyans to confront one of the uglier vestiges of colonial rule, ethnicity.

The metal scene in Kenya is still young, vibrant and slowly learning how to engage with the world around them. My visits to the country have informed me of the local bands' alacrity to push forward, to embrace the world around them, and to shed their colonial legacies once and for all. This final chapter will also look at how music was able to endure through various facets of their post-colonial experience, as well as how rock music was able to gain a foothold in the modern Kenyan state. Through the tumult of authoritarianism and any variety of economic difficulties, the modern rock and metal scenes exist by dint of the endurance of those that came before them, whether or not the current generation is even aware of what existed in previous generations.

A note on culture and tradition

Throughout this book I use the terms 'culture' and 'tradition', neither of which I mean to use as interchangeable descriptors. Cultures are local norms. They are not static. They are living, breathing entities shaped by people and time, defined by their common histories. Western ideas of cultures are quite often linked to a romantic idea of what our expectations are, not what reality shows.

Post-colonial cultures, however, are still shaped by lingering vestiges that have transformed their economic, political and religious makeup. Populations located in the Global South remain attached to a colonial entity as a result of the era of colonial expansion. Notably in Africa, governments are dependent on the global economy, firmly attached to their former colonial partners for trade and goods, as well as those of their neighbouring nations, who also tether themselves to Western markets. Inevitably, culture is also linked to the West for other variables of entertainment, which includes music.

Whether or not post-colonial cultures seek to redefine themselves in a manner that separate from their colonial history, they will do so under a matrix of post-colonialism, not pre-colonialism, as too much has changed in the lives of sub-Saharan Africans for cultures to been reverted to pre-colonial life. Thus, I am intending to identify the culture and norms that the musicians have grown up with, and the patterns and ways associated with their lives in their countries of today.

Tradition is the way you understand things to be, how you were taught to do them or what is 'customary' to the individual. Traditions are the agreed-upon thoughts and ways within a societal grouping that exist to form boundaries of celebrations, entertainment, passages of time, births, deaths and unifications (marriages). Culture is what encompasses these norms.

Throughout this book, I use the term 'traditional' and define 'traditions' as the approach taken to their norms and routines in their everyday, modern lives. I am saying this because I also believe that traditions are in motion, always evolving and adapting while retaining certain aspects of their origins, notably for frequent occurrences (such as birthdays). And, because I believe that African 'traditions' were greatly affected by the arrivals of not only colonial governments but also religious missionaries, I have chosen to accept that traditions are in fact linear. As Sean Mallon says:

> One of the key problems with the way 'tradition' is used is that it implies an evolu-tionary linear progression from the past to the present, but there is also a timeless-ness associated with the term. 'Tradition' can be used to conveniently describe a 'non-time-specific' way of life. People talk about 'traditional' societies and practices as if they are somehow pure and untouched by the outside world.

(2010: 364)

The reason I feel that traditional practices are this way in modern Africa is because cultures have to interact with their settings, whether organic or imported – as is the case in former colonial nations. It is these interactions which are required when it comes to understanding the work of musicians, and, as such, they can only be understood with personal interactions.

What is presented in the following pages is how heavy metal (and hard rock) music and its global sub-culture fits into these African settings and the manner in which this sub-culture has been acclimated to not only its participants but also Westerners viewing this scene from afar.

PART I

HEAVY METAL
AND CULTURAL
CONFRONTATIONS

1

Arka'n Asrafokor and the
Reinvention of Togo

If there ever is a measure to test one's patience, a great start would have been the soundcheck the members of the metal band Arka'n Asrafokor found themselves enduring on 20 September 2019. Situated just minutes from Lomé, Togo's capital city centre, the Level Cultural Centre, an outdoor venue where the band was set to perform that night, became the focal point of their morning, afternoon and evening. They sat, they waited, they made phone calls, they kept taking walks between the front of the house and the soundboard, as well as paces outside of the venue for the sake of venting frustrations as the day dragged on.

This task of arriving at the venue, setting up equipment, adjusting sound levels and ensuring that everything sounded well in the front of the house (and on the stage) for the incoming audience is standard practice for bands worldwide. However, it is not likely that any metal band in the world would have to endure the marathon soundcheck that Arka'n Asrafokor did for their performance.

Having skipped breakfast at home to ensure they arrived on time at 10 a.m., there was already a lingering hunger as everyone assumed this process would take no more than 30 minutes. There was to be no lunch break, nor dinner break for that matter. If there was ever a moment to understand the Western colloquialism 'everything that could possibly go wrong, will go wrong', this was it. Cables, amplifiers, speakers, soundboards – all would malfunction at some point during that soundcheck. Employees of the hired sound company were tasked with chasing down functioning equipment and accessories from anyone they knew in Lomé and returning with them to the venue a significant amount of time later, including a staffer that came back clutching a rather large speaker on the back of a motorcycle taxi (see Figure 1.1). In Togo, necessity determines possibilities.

None of the band members left the venue throughout the day, including Arka'n Asrafokor's drummer Richard, who quietly and patiently sat behind the drum set at the venue for the duration of the afternoon. Never did Richard complain to anyone about being hungry, thirsty or impatient. Another band member, percussionist Mass, would take a nap on stage, oblivious to the

FIGURE 1.1: An employee of the Level Cultural Centre returns with a speaker on the back of a motorcycle taxi, 2019. Photo by the author.

employees still setting up the lights for the evening and the sponsors who wanted to make sure their ads would be seen in as many possible photographs from the event, not waking even from the sound of an amplified seven-stringed guitar at full volume being performed through the speakers. Mass was exhausted. Bassist Francis would periodically appear only to disappear, while keyboard player and co-vocalist Enrico was the one fortunate member who was finishing up exams for a university course he was taking (arriving at the venue just as the band hit the stage that evening).

The entire soundcheck took nine hours.

Arka'n Asrafokor's event that evening was free of charge to the public, a necessary detail in order to attract an audience in this cash-strapped nation. The band's frontman Rock (he prefers to be quoted by this name, which he has had for most of his life) organized the event upon hearing of my planned visit to the country, as he not only wanted to showcase his band's music in front of an audience but also wanted me to better understand the band's difficulties in performing metal in Togo – though the nine-hour soundcheck was never a part of the plan. Part of what kept Rock focused throughout the ordeal was his relentless pursuit of perfection: a visionary with a mindset that was never guarded, as his drive is on display full-time. During the soundcheck, Rock was stationed behind the soundboard making sure the technician who was set to work their sound that evening was well aware of what he was going to do that night. To him, Arka'n Asrafokor's sound could not be compromised.

There were two notable reasons I was in Togo. First, Arka'n Asrafokor were the first heavy metal band I had come across in a West African nation. While I was aware of the growing interest in rock and metal in Nigeria, I was surprised to find a band that had come out of Togo, notably because of the likely difficulties that such a band would face in a nation where just over half of the population lives in poverty (World Bank 2019a). With the exception of fieldwork carried out in Madagascar and Reunion Island, whose scenes are quite deep and impressively well organized, the dearth of output from the continent's French legacies is rather surprising.

Secondly, and most importantly, what grabs listeners hearing Arka'n Asrafokor's music for the first time is their approach of articulating a hybrid that melded the sounds and languages of Togo within the framework of a heavy metal band. This chapter takes a closer look at the latter, the musical hybridity, or the infusion, of two rather contrasting cultural stamps into one: heavy metal and Togolese music. I will demonstrate how Arka'n Asrafokor has brought together these two styles and why musical hybridity matters in the postcolonial continent. Relying on both primary sources through fieldwork as well as secondary sources, this chapter will also examine Togo and its postcolonial political history that has shaped the way Arka'n Asrafokor has been able to deliver their music and how it is being viewed by Westerners. Can cultural infusions from metal bands in the Global South be viewed equally within the greater rubric of heavy metal? Or, should non-White, non-Western acts be labelled differently because of more traditional approaches?

There is a rather unique precedent to these cultural infusions by way of Brazilian heavy metal giants Sepultura and their seminal album *Roots* (1996). In this chapter, I will also highlight some comparisons between Arka'n Asrafokor and Sepultura for the sake of arguing that the latter's was an inauthentic venture of convenience that helped the band catapult their career, whereas Arka'n Asrafokor's intentions are an expression of authenticity that reflects who they are and where they are from. If any band in the continent could carry the term 'African heavy metal' well, it would be Arka'n Asrafokor (see Figure 1.2). Their music is powerful as a result of this intrinsic aspect, leaving an impression and stamp that no other band in the African continent had yet to tap into.

Furthermore, I argue that this interaction between Western and traditional forms of music is an approach that epitomizes how decolonialism also can be embraced by heavy metal as the band's musical interpretations are reclamations. Noting that their music is a response to Togo's French colonial history, they challenge what is not only possible within the audio aspects of the genre but also feature lyrical content that seeks a reclamation of a pre-colonial Togo, which the band members attribute firmly to their culture, their spirituality and their land.

15

FIGURE 1.2: Arka'n Asrafokor in 2019. Left to right: Richard, Rock, Mass, Francis and Enrico. Photo courtesy of Arka'n Asrafokor.

Bridging hope

Arka'n Asrafokor are the only heavy metal band in Togo. The salient reason the sound engineers and employees setting up the performance that evening had struggled was because they had never confronted heavy metal before. Rock music, too, was a rare find in this nation, however, it was not entirely out of the Togolese market. Rock notes that this type of music was heard in modicum on radio stations, with some in the country also owning cassettes of well-established Western rock acts (likely bootlegged copies). Citing Led Zeppelin, The Scorpions and Guns N' Roses as albums he heard growing up, Rock indicated that there also had been another local artist that he heard a lot growing up on the radio, one that he labelled as a rock artist. His name was Jimi Hope.

Born Koffi Senaya, Jimi Hope is well revered among musicians in Togo as a pioneer whose contributions to Togolese music are immeasurable. Known as 'Togo's rocker', his engagement with Togolese society during a difficult period for the country – 'an environment culturally neglected by the state, yet unambiguously laden with the threat of an ever-present government' (Saibou 2016: 117) – allowed Hope to endure when no one else would dare. His Westward reach helped musicians in the country realize that there was more they could do to add new sounds to their art. Madeline Saibou says that Hope's interest in rock music was spurred by accessing the hotels and clubs Westerners frequented and simply asking who their favourite artists were, and getting copies of the music the DJs were playing for Westerners onto cassettes for a small fee (2016: 122).

Adapting his moniker after one of his favourite artists, Jimi Hendrix, Hope understood his place in the greater Togolese music scene. Arka'n Asrafokor knows this well too – understanding that they also are occupying a solitary space in their nation of seven million (as the only group performing a certain type of music) and that they, too, are using a type of music that has not fully engaged with the Togolese populace to better articulate their cultural place and understanding of the world. Hope used his music to further explore his African identity, as he grew to understand that the blues-influenced Western form of music he enjoyed and performed had African roots (Saibou 2016: 128).

I was looking forward to meeting and interviewing him during my trip to Togo. Sadly, Hope passed away a few weeks before my scheduled visit. However, spending the time I did in Lomé, I was able to get a sense of the musical legacy he had left for aspiring musicians in the country. Reminiscing on the friendship he had developed with Hope, Rock informed me that Hope's presence in the Togolese music culture was immeasurable. Yet, given Hope's presence and fanbase, the members of Arka'n Asrafokor were provided with a glimmer of hope that a space was now open for this type of music to gain validation in their country.

Formed in 2009 as Arka'n (they added Asrafokor[1] in 2020), their music during its early period was rough, derivative and without direction. Furthermore, forming a heavy metal band in Togo was not easy: bands in the country typically do not form for the sake of pursuing creative ambitions, as most groups form for a specific performance with a payment in mind. Performing for a few years with a lineup that included Rock, his brother and co-vocalist Enrico alongside two other members that they considered close friends, Rock had set his sights on a more ambitious sound. While this early incarnation of the band struggled through like most bands, Rock was also performing in another band called Rock On, playing covers of contemporary hits around Lomé for the extra income. When he needed to replace the original members of the band who departed in 2015, he turned to Rock On's bassist Francis and drummer Richard. The addition of these two sat well with the brothers, as Francis and Richard proved to be great due to their enjoyment of metal as well as an understanding of what it means to be in a band for the sake of pursuing a vision (Enrico 2019).

For Rock, an artist fixated on perfection, what challenged him more than anything during this transition was how to pursue the music he had imagined for the band. His ideas were different and quite unlike anything he had ever heard himself in heavy metal, nor anything that had ever been recorded. What Rock envisioned was a reinvention of the music he had been exposed to his whole life while still focusing on the more aggressive metal sounds he had embraced as an adult. Arka'n Asrafokor, in his mind, was to be an extension of life in Togo through music. The reborn lineup was also on board.

The four members had decided that adding a Togolese percussionist would benefit the band and assist them in carrying out their vision for the music. In 2016, they enlisted percussionist and co-vocalist Mass to complete the vision. Though the members of the band had known Mass locally as a rapper, they knew he was also well versed on Togolese percussion instruments, having previously performed in a traditional ensemble. However, as the members suspected, Mass' inclusion provided a challenge at first, as percussionists in Togo are not accustomed to performing within set structures of crafted songs – building melodies, separating those melodies from verses, bridges, breakdowns, introductions or dramatic pauses. However, Mass proved himself quickly, embracing the band's vision with flourishing results.

The addition of Mass allowed the band to bridge a style of heavy metal already familiar to fans worldwide with Togolese music that is otherwise unfamiliar to audiences outside the nation. This chosen interaction between Togolese music and the genre of heavy metal is a form of hybridization, a combining of not only two musical ideas but also of two disparate ideological circumstances, as each style of music represented an ethos: Togolese music representing a cultural celebration, while heavy metal stood as a representation against the status quo. Was this inevitable in Africa? As Martin Stokes argues, yes. 'If the global circulation of music had, until the relatively recent past, taken place in a space defined by colonialism and its aftermath [...] the same cannot be said now', as varying musical cultures are in closer contact by way of increased mobility between populations as well as increasing access to various forms of media (Stokes 2008: 6). Hybridization works because traditions, like music, are not truly static. They both exist in constant motion, adaptable and open to interpretation. Much like ideas and lived memories, traditions, and music are what a culture uses to inform what else is possible.

The members of Arka'n Asrafokor belong to the Ewe ethnic group, which accounts for one-third of the Togolese population. Primarily situated in the southern, coastal portion of the country, Ewe communities are also found in eastern Ghana and Benin. United by a history and a language, this division of Ewe between nations is a result of the colonial maps drawn by Europeans. Little is known of Ewe history, though 'oral tradition tells of Ewe flight from a brutal seventeenth-century tyrant, King Agokole of Notsé' (O'Malley 2010: 454).

Historian Martin Meredith notes that perhaps little is known of Ewe history because, like other groups in West Africa, notably the Igbo and Yoruba of Nigeria, Ewe were also a colonial product by way of missionary endeavours, who would transcribe various hitherto unwritten languages into written form, thus reducing the number of spoken languages to fewer written languages in order to clearly define linguistic groups and subsequently tribes. 'Missionaries were also active in documenting local customs and traditions and in compiling "tribal histories" which were then incorporated into the curricula of their mission schools, spreading the notion of tribal identity' (Meredith 2014: 519–20).

One thing that is a matter of pride for Ewe culture is music. This full embrace of their home culture is the salient aspect that separates Arka'n Asrafokor from other African metal bands by incorporating the *djembe* (a type of drum), a *gankogui* (a local cowbell; see Figure 1.3), *axatse* (a percussive shaker), *Evù* drums and the West African talking drum into their music. This collision between tradition and Western derives from the instrumentation they have known their whole lives, representing a concerted effort to perform this type of music in their own accent (Rock 2019).

Austin Emielu writes about the collision between Western musical forms and African music, and the process behind the creation of new forms is characterized by two forms of social and cultural aspects: indigenization or syncretization (2011: 385). The use of traditional music by Arka'n Asrafokor could be seen as a form of indigenization, or 'the reworking of and adaptation of otherwise foreign musical forms to reflect cultural and aesthetic benchmarks that are essentially African' (Emielu 2011: 385). By reworking Togolese instrumentation with distorted seven-stringed guitars as well as double-bass drum patterns, what they are doing could also be seen as a form of syncretization, a 'creative mixture of foreign and traditional African musical resources to create new forms of "syncretic music"' (Emielu 2011: 385).

As John O'Flynn writes, 'hybridization is a concept that tends to be associated with the postmodern condition of globality' (2007: 34), or a scenario in which

FIGURE 1.3: Mass during a rehearsal in 2019. Note the *gankoguis* ('cowbells') he is performing. Photo by the author.

a colonial subject can now occupy a space within a greater context than the local, which is very much what Arka'n Asrafokor is doing insomuch as they are seeking validation from a global audience for their effort. Furthermore, O'Flynn adds, 'globalization tends to regard hybridity and syncretism as an antidote to essential notions of identity and ethnicity' (2007: 34). In this way, by using heavy metal as an expression of themselves and who they are, Arka'n Asrafokor is using their music to construct a new national identity for themselves – a reinvention of Togo. They have gone beyond negotiating their sound for an authentic representation of who they are and they have chosen to represent their identity (Stokes cited in O'Flynn 2007: 33) as a heavy metal band.

Hybridization here must also be argued as a concept beyond music. It is also a cultural melding, an amalgamation of two disparate ideas: heavy metal as a philosophy rooted in rebellion, while tradition, in this case Ewe, is tethered to its own set of norms and standards. This is what Arka'n Asrafokor are redefining – what these two cultures can look like in motion together. They are envisioning a new Togo, a new Ewe, reflecting their culture in an ever-changing, capitalist-driven world that seldom tolerates antiquated traditions.

As discussed in the previous chapter, hybridity is also shaped 'by settings as much as it can be informed by cultural forms' (Lull 2000: 242–43). Arka'n Asrafokor's place in modern Togolese society is very much an interpretation of what they are living through politically and socially, connecting every circumstance, emotion and modern tradition together to a past they were raised to inherit in a distinct, authentic hybrid.

Greetings from the third world

Outside of Africa, the melding of traditional infusions into heavy metal has provided plenty of examples of bands that have embraced local sounds and themes into their music. Heavy metal bands from diverse corners of the world such as Finland's Korpikalaani, Latvia's Skyforger, Taiwan's Chthonic, Palestine's Melechesh, Israel's Orphaned Land, Kentucky's Panopticon and Brazil's Sepultura, have all, in various capacities, infused lyrical or musical heritage into their sounds, whether through the experimentation of an album or as a defining characteristic of their music.

Sepultura, a thrash metal band formed in Belo Horizonte, Brazil, in the mid 1980s, has become the primary example in the metal world of a band that bridged the sounds of the pre-colonial and modernity with the release of their seminal 1996 album *Roots*. Described as their 'rediscovery of Brazil' (Avelar 2003: 333), *Roots* features performances of the Xavante, an indigenous group from the nation's

Amazon rainforest region, as well as other variations of musical stylings that harken to the country's slave trade.

For the members of Sepultura, all of whom are Brazilians of European descent, to approach an indigenous group in their country in an innocuous and respectful manner took an extraordinary amount of patience and was a leap forward that has still not been replicated in heavy metal. The interaction came by way of the band's then-vocalist Max Cavalera's sense of wanting to understand his country's indigenous groups after watching a transformation of a character in a film titled *At Play in the Fields of the Lord* (Babenco 1991). Enlisting the help of Brazil's Indigenous Culture Center, Sepultura (alongside the album's American producer, Ross Robinson), found themselves travelling via four Cessna airplanes into the Xavante's homeland (Reyes-Kulkarni 2016) with some recording equipment and a few acoustic instruments. Granted permission by the head of the Xavante group, the band recorded an interpretation that the group performed using only a chant, adding a layer of acoustic guitars and percussion, an exchange captured on the album's track 'Istári' (Sepultura 1996).

This exchange proved to be a positive one, as anthropologist Laura R. Graham notes; it was a manner in which they were able to bring awareness to their plight and to share their music with a new audience.

> The Xavante want to be known and they want their culture to be known. They want their music to be known because they think it's beautiful and view it as a contribution to humanity. It's like, 'We have something beautiful to contribute to humanity—and, by the way, here we are suffering. We want people to know who we are and that we exist'. And so when they got this proposal from a musical group that wanted to come jam and share music with them, they loved it.
>
> (Graham cited in Reyes-Kulkarni 2016: n.pag.)

Similarly, another track on *Roots*, 'Ratamahatta' (Sepultura 1996) explores a different aspect of the band's awareness of a struggle within their nation, focusing on the plight of the nation's slum dwellers. The only song on the record performed in the band's native Portuguese is driven by an incredibly powerful rhythm and is a remarkable mix of varying musical cultures and instrumentation that resulted from the country's slave trade. As Idelber Avelar says:

> This is a song that features not only the usual metal rhythm section, distorted guitars and hoarse loud vocals but also Amazonian Xavante singing and a percussion ensemble made up of large bass drums (the *surdo*, used in samba, maracatu and other Brazilian/Afrodiasporic genres), cans, djembes, water tanks and rattles, all played by Brazilian percussion wizard, multimedia figure and activist, Carlinhos Brown.

The track opens with Xavante vocals over drumming in 2/4 time, accompanied by the metallic sound of a shaker.

(Avelar 2003: 338, original emphasis)

This song also employs the use of a *maracatu* rhythm, a pre-colonial African sound that has been appropriated into Brazilian culture and is readily heard and enjoyed by Brazilians every year as part of their famed Carnival celebrations. Among the instruments used to perform the rhythm of the song are a *gonguê*, a metal cowbell, and a *xequerê* or *agbê,* a gourd shaker wrapped in beads, all of which are instruments with African origins. The use of these instruments is significant as it ties the performance of one heavy metal's venerated acts, one that hails from the Global South, to West Africa.

Arka'n Asrafokor's music often draws comparisons to the work of the Brazilian metal stalwarts. It is a comparison they receive often from fans all over the world because of the success the *Roots* album garnered, catapulting Sepultura to a level of success that has cemented their legacy. Rock explains that he does not mind these comparisons, noting that the Brazilians responsible for bringing these instruments to the new world 'were deported from Africa', however, he states that the band's goal is to keep their music and their sound true to their visions, and ultimately, to have Arka'n Asrafokor's music stand on its own. '*We* already are what *we* are', he adds (Rock 2019: n.pag., original emphasis).

What Sepultura did with this album (after a significant lineup change, the band would return to their thrash origins) was establish an expectation of what heavy metal from the Global South could sound like, what I refer to as the '*Roots* effect' – an expectation placed on artists from the Global South to 'other' themselves because 'they' are from somewhere 'exotic' or 'different' from 'us'. Sepultura reached towards the 'other', towards an 'exotic' sound, for inspiration within their borders likely because it provided them with the opportunity to present something that was 'otherwise unusual' for foreign audiences (Williams and Da Rocha 2017: 147). But, as Keith Kahn-Harris says, the band who once performed music to stray from their Brazilian origins embraced their 'Brazilianess' upon relocating to the United States (Kahn-Harris 2000: 14).

Relying on traditional music to push forth your message asks whether or not what Arka'n Asrafokor is doing works to promulgate a cultural or counter-cultural stance, because rock and metal musicians in Africa have only, in modicum, relied on their traditions as a musical source of inspiration. Without question, African rock and metal acts rely on lived experiences for lyrical inspirations, but musically there is little heard that indicates African origins. Where Sepultura reached towards the 'other' within their borders to better articulate their vision for an album, the members of Arka'n Asrafokor took a step into their own personal history, relying on a Western form of music to better articulate their traditions. In doing so, they too, invited Western listeners into the Global South.

Zã Keli

It was during the *Berlin Conference* that this narrow slip of a country was drawn. Once known as the Slave Coast, Togoland (as it was then referred to) was penned on German maps in 1884 as a new protectorate, which also included a portion of modern Ghana's eastern Volta region. With European traders already well acquainted with the region as a result of their interest in human capital, Germany had taken a strong interest in other resources the nation had to offer: notably cotton, cocoa and coffee. Between the 9th and 26th of August in 1914, during the First World War, Germany found itself fighting British and French forces who had invaded the country in what was known as the Togoland Campaign, after which Germany conceded control of the colony to the European nations that would once again carve up the nation in 1922, with the western portion known as British Togoland[2] and France gaining what would become the modern Togo until the nation's independence in April 1960.

Togo's political history began with the curiosity of having its first president, Sylvanus Olympio, win the country's debut election with 99 per cent of the vote (*New York Times* 1961), which was the convenient result of his banishment of any political opponents during his tenure as Togo's premier. Two years later his exiled opponents returned to the country and assassinated him while he stood in front of the American embassy, making Togo the first African state to be rattled by a coup d'état (Mazrui 1968: 40–41). The man who shot Olympio, Gnassingbé Eyadéma, became the president of Togo in 1967, serving in the position until his death in 2005.[3]

Eyadéma's leadership was remembered for the attention he enjoyed placing on himself, the epitome of a true 'Big Man'. His personality and his nepotism took centre stage as his rule was validated by an army made up of his Kabiyé people, known for their servility to him, enforcing a single-party rule and suppressing political dissent by way of torture. As historian John Iliffe writes, Eyadéma's cult of personality stemmed greatly from his surviving an airplane crash (there were others who survived, yet his story depended on the lie that he was the sole survivor), thus validating a 'divine deliverance from imperialist conspiracy' (2005: 333). This heroic account of survival and endurance ultimately led to 'Eyadema-ism – the veneration of his patriotism and the codification of his ideas' (Iliffe 2005: 333) to be understood as a national ideology. His images are ubiquitously depicted throughout the nation in statues as well as the preservation of the site of the plane crash where he 'miraculously' survived. Eyadéma's rule served as the archetype for simulacrums that followed in the post-colonial Africa, leaders whose names and nations become metonyms for their bombastic knavery – Mobotu Sese Soko's Congo, Idi Amin's Uganda, Daniel arap Moi's Kenya, Sekou Toure's Guinea and

Robert Mugabe's Zimbabwe – despots who ruled through myth as much as they ruled by wielding unrelenting, unchecked power.

Eyadéma's son, Faure Gnassingbé, was sworn in as President the day following his father's death, a job he will likely hold for the duration of his life, too. It is under this rubric of corruption, nepotism and illiberalism that the members of Arka'n Asrafokor live. The Togo that exists now is a skeleton of what it once was: a country in name only. Enrico insists that culturally things were better immediately after the departure of the colonial government because there was stronger respect for traditional culture, whereas today's Togolese are continually looking French-ward. 'People used to think like human beings. The culture was still in front of everything. But now they destroy it […] we don't care about the respect of it. All we want now, it is more about the capitalism', he says, adding that, in his view, music in Togo has become a carbon copy, or a mimicry of what is occurring in the Global North (Enrico 2019: n.pag.).

Most of the music heard on the local radio stations was standard-fare pop, including the top hits from international artists as well as a few other songs from Togolese artists. Local pop music was performed in Ewe, other times in French and, in rare instances, English. Pop music, like anywhere else in the world, dominates Togolese airwaves. Enrico's frustration with local music exists because he feels that the Togolese are too distracted by 'ass and breast' (Enrico 2019: n.pag.) music to pay attention to the deteriorating of their traditions. Togolese author Abiadé Basil Adéwusi also argues that the nation is losing its way musically as a result of the 'admiration of, and reliance on, imported music styles, for which he blamed the public's preferences and behaviour, especially a dismissive attitude towards the local cultural heritage' (cited in Saibou 2016: 111). Much of this stems from colonialism and the way that colonial governments tricked their subjects into a continual game of 'mimicry' (Bhabha 1984: 128–29) in which colonial subjects were led to believe that living, acting and sounding like their colonizers was the pinnacle of behaviour.

Colonialism's construction was not only a model for European nations to enforce economic superiority but also a manner in which to construct social and cultural superiority. The danger in colonial repetition was that colonial subjects believed they were inferior unless they adapted the ways of their colonizers. In his celebrated work, *Black Skin, White Masks*, decolonial thinker Frantz Fanon says:

> All colonized people – on other words, people in whom an inferiority complex has taken root, whose local cultural originality has been committed to the grave – position themselves in relation to the civilizing language: i.e., the metropolitan culture. The more the colonized has assimilated the cultural values of the metropolis, the more he will have escaped the bush.
>
> (2008: 2)

Culturally, the Togolese live vicariously through their former colonial masters. When Enrico spoke of the cultural erosion that has occurred by way of music, what he was alluding to was 'cultural imperialism', a form of influencing a society by the overreaching popular culture of another, notably more prominent, society. Bolivian writer Luis Ramiro Beltran defines cultural imperialism as 'a verifiable process of social influence by which a nation imposes on other countries its set of beliefs, values, knowledge, and behavioural norms as well as its overall style of life' (1978: 184). This 'indiscriminate dumping' (Tunstall 1977: 57) generally does not include heavy metal, however. Nor would I argue that metal could be a form of cultural imperialism for the reason that it has only been seen as viable for those that embrace a subculture that is far too often marginalized. Metal fans have embraced the subculture because it resembles nothing like the 'play-it-safe' life that is seemingly out of reach, and out of touch for those looking to turn new corners.

What the band has done for their Togolese listeners is reach beyond the distractions of the contemporary world and step closer to their pre-colonial cultural heritages while confronting their postcolonial identity, which is not something pop music invokes, as metal scenes often 'prod the boundaries of "normalcy" and promote non-conformity through both their countercultural unity and their rebellious musical styles and lyrical themes' (Hendricks 2017: 121).

Heavy metal and hard rock have shaped the lives of the members of Arka'n Asrafokor because what they heard was nothing like the standard fare of play-it-safe pop and, thus, not a form of mimicry of Western ambition – especially French life. This was the music that represented those whose existence lay in challenging political and societal norms as it best reflected mindsets of rejection.

Lyrically, Arka'n Asrafokor have stepped into their pre-colonial culture for inspiration and are doing so without fomenting any political activism, much in the same fashion that is being performed by heavy metal acts in Puerto Rico, whose positions rely less on political motivations and more so on 'stances of its cultural life' (Varas-Díaz et al. 2019: 238). As Varas-Díaz et al. identify, this trend of citing pre-colonial themes is steadily found throughout their case studies among metal bands in Latin America as well.

Two songs from Arka'n Asrafokor's 2019 album *Zã Keli* highlight their cultural stances well: 'Warrior Song' and 'Tears of the Dead', both of which feature lyrics in English and Ewe. By stepping away from the colonial language (they do perform in French in modicum on a few moments throughout the album) the listener is provided with an entry point in which they manage the presentation of their culture, their history and their 'contents in terms of thought and forms of knowledge' (Sarr 2019: 76). This gesture could also be understood as a step into comfort of ownership, as by abandoning the genre's *lingua franca* they are not only sending a more confident and personal message to fans around the world but they are also recognizing their home audience (Wallach cited in Lee 2018: 534).

Discussing 'Warrior Song' (Arka'n Asrafokor 2019), Rock says that the band purposefully placed the song as the album's opening track because of the song's lyrical relevance to their culture, one that existed long before the French began hovering over their lives. The song opens with the distinct sound of the *gankogui*, a cowbell-like instrument that is performed by Mass in a 6/8 time signature, as a clean guitar line performs the song's Ewe rhythm in a lead intro, roping the listener in before being joined by the rest of the band in a distorted seven-stringed guitar pummeling. Through a remarkably heavy and catchy riff, listeners who may have otherwise been roped in by the sounds of an African rhythm are quickly shown that this is a heavy metal record as 'Warrior Song' explodes into a harmonious spectacle of moveable rhythms and multi-layered vocals. Once the lyrics commence with Rock's clean vocals, the band accompanies him throughout the verse of the song with a unison-led group chant in their native Ewe – 'Ooo ŋsɛ̃tɔ, kalẽawo fofu loo/Be natsɔ dziɖuɖu na wo' ('Ooh! Almighty! Warriors gather at your feet asking for power and victory') – before giving way to Enrico's fiery rapping over the song's guiding melody:

> I am standing right here with my fist in the air,
> Looking at the sun drying my tears at noon.
> Man (Chaley) here with my brothers,
> Walking with no fear.
> Cuz He talks to the elements,
> Walking before us
>
> (Arka'n Asrafokor 2019)

Rock explains that their God is not like one that is often associated as a central figure in an organized religion. Rather theirs is an omniscient presence alive throughout the natural elements: earth, fire, wind and water. The song, which is typically their opening song during live performances, also serves as a summoning:

> In the past all of the warriors know about everything, like they know how to communicate with plants and the Earth. So all of the elements work with him. So we put this as the first song of the album, like we are going to war – 'Warrior Song'. We invite the elements of the Warrior to accompany us.
>
> (Rock 2019: n.pag.)

'Warrior Song' exemplifies decolonialism, as it beckons its local listeners to think about the lives of their ancestors as well as what life meant to the Ewe before the arrival of missionaries, slave traders and French colonialists.

Likewise 'Tears of the Dead' (Arka'n Asrafokor 2019) is reaching towards nature and culture as inspiration. For this track, the band also released a video to serve as a promotion for their album. The band, who present themselves with white body paint across their arms and faces to portray the look of warriors, performed the song in a wooded area amidst flames to striking effect, delivering a video that makes an immediate impression on viewers as it centres the band in their Togolese setting. Viewers may also note Enrico's use of chains bonding his hands, an unpleasant reminder of the pain their ancestors – from the country once known as the Slave Coast – endured during the Middle Passages. Much like 'Warrior Song', 'Tears of the Dead' commences with a percussive rhythm, with Mass simultaneously accompanied by Richard performing the song's introduction with a *shekere*, a gourd-shaped instrument wrapped in beads that produce a distinct sound when the instrument is shaken. This introduction spans nine seconds before giving way to the electric guitar and drums, and, once again, a chanting performed in Ewe. 'Tears of the Dead' is far more aggressive than many of the others songs from the album, notably because of Richard breaking into a machine-gun-like double-bass drum pattern and Enrico's deep guttural approach to the vocals on the song, both emblematic of the band's more aggressive influences.

In the video, the audience is shown images of deceased children (they are actors – no one was harmed) in a forest, and a man who comes across them in disbelief before walking away into a separate area of the forest, kneeling and praying. Viewers follow the man, who is revealed to be a priest, seeking an offering. At the 2:10 mark of the video, viewers meet the spirit of a woman who appears in a ceremonious dance. Shortly thereafter the woman transforms after being struck by a lightning bolt, her eyes sinking deep into the back of her head while turning an ashen white. The children who we encountered earlier are now huddled, zombie-like, marching towards the camera while the woman continues to undergo her transformation. Some of the children are seen rising as shadows, ascending skyward over the backdrop of the dark forest from which they emerged while other children are shown engaging in a ceremony, waving their hands behind a tree with their faces obscured as if they were shadows – the distorted guitars sit back entirely out of the mix. The only member of the band in focus performing at this point is Mass. Viewers are locked into him as he performs a traditional, almost ritualistic section of the song. Just before this section arrives, the band performs the following lyrics in Ewe in prelude:

Nɔviwoe, vu kɔɖi sɔgbɔ do gu anyigba kple vi maɖifõwo
Nyatefe Anyigba la ke nu bia akɔta wo.
Heeeyia, tso kufia nawo
Heee kalɛawo fɔ, ŋɔliawo fɔ, dzatawo fɔ!!!

27

('Brothers, the blood of too many innocent children has been shed cursing the land
In truth I tell you
Earth will open up her mouth and will judge them
Will condemn them
Warriors are rising, the dead are rising, lions are rising').

(Arka'n Asrafokor 2019)

This ceremony and unveiling of the woman was portrayed by the band as a way to connect the viewers with their culture directly. Rock says the children in the video were shown to be killed but the viewers are not shown how. They, like the priest, are saddened by their appearance, and his prayer is a summoning of the Earth. The woman, or spirit, was summoned by the priest and revealed to be Mother Earth, who is disappointed to learn of what has happened to her children, thereby instructing the priest to change his faith – to relinquish the Western faith and once again take up a pre-missionary faith – in order to heal: the 'Priest is calling Mother Earth to wake up, to destroy those who killed the children' (Rock 2019: n.pag.), an allegory that man and nature must not be at war, but rather in harmony with each other.

Rock had also asked the band to perform a new song that they had been working on in the previous weeks during one of their rehearsals, one that was being composed for their next album. The song, which was still unnamed at the time of this writing, was led by Mass on vocals and performed in Ewe. Rock informed me that this song was perhaps the most political they had composed yet. He had guided me to this song in particular after I inquired whether any of their songs addressed current events. Rock explained that this song was a warning to humans of the destruction of the planet that we are collectively occupying, asking for their God to punish those who punish his Earth, our Earth. 'In this song, we implore him to unchain all his rage against all those who spoil him, disrespect him, and we ask Him to take them off his surface with no mercy', says Rock (2019: n.pag.).

These examples not only highlight how Arka'n Asrafokor has embraced their locality by using the Earth, a central part of Ewe culture, as a theme in some of their lyrics, but also how they are able to take control over their situation, their culture and their history. This is a powerful reclamation for the band. Colonial rule ensured that Africans were not African: Your gods were not to be worshipped, your languages were not to be spoken, your norms were watered down and eventually forgotten. African culture – literature, arts, poetry and music – suffered because of this, as Africans were inculcated into believing their articulations of life were no good. This is the narrative that Arka'n Asrafokor hopes to destroy because in Rock's view (with the nodding approval of his bandmates gathered around) cultural control is a manner of securing 'superiority' (Rock 2019). Metal fits their life and their narrative because it best reflects the expression that they are trying to convey to non-Western and especially Western audiences alike. And, as Rock emphatically argues, the band has a strong connection to metal because this music belongs to them in more ways than one:

Rock [music] comes from Africa and if you listen to our patterns [mimes metal drum patterns], it's metal! There's no difference. Metal came from Africa, travels to the (United States) and then goes to England. For me, metal comes from Africa, that's why it's so easy for me to blend the inspiration to both music [...] it is part of our past culture. So, how ridiculous it is [to] tell a people that you are not allowed to express who you originally are.

(Rock 2019: n.pag.)

Sharing this knowledge in their language has allowed Arka'n Asrafokor the privilege of sharing an experience with Western listeners that otherwise may have been understood through the lens of stereotypes. This is the reclamation of their Africa, the 'real Africa', one that Enrico, also rather emphatically, notes is necessary for them to get back, and to change, the Africa that they envision through their music: 'where humanity, honour, respect of life have a meaning [...] And we have to take actions to change the perception the others have; Remember the warriors we are' (Enrico 2019: n.pag.).

This embrace is an organic compromise between their interest in performing heavy metal as well as their proclivities to celebrate their culture, their upbringing and their country without having to reach into the 'other' Senegalese decolonial scholar Felwine Sarr says: 'This act of speaking for oneself, of being simultaneously critical of Western knowledge regarding Africa but just as critical of the knowledge discourses that Africans hold onto in regard of their history and their own culture is of the utmost importance' (2019: 75).

Musically, rock and heavy metal have grown accustomed to an audible standard of what is rock and metal, or its 'code' (Avelar 2011: 138) as the genre has been identified quite often by its presence of distorted guitars, attacking rhythm sections and if not an overtly aggressive vocal style, aggressive vocal approaches. This distinctive sound 'became codified and crystallized after its formative period' (Weinstein 2000: 37) in the British midlands in the early 1970s with the release of Black Sabbath's debut album. Lyrically, the genre has been able to step away from the distractions that other, more popular forms of music provide as early on heavy metal, notably with Black Sabbath, tackled macabre, anti-war themes. In essence, Black Sabbath's arrival served as a template for what could be possible within the confines of this genre as a result of the honesty of expression that could be provided within the framework of extreme music. However, it must be reiterated that Black Sabbath's sound is also a hybridization of the band's influences, notably American-rooted blues, classical music and early rock 'n' roll. And though it served as a template for what else could be possible musically, Black Sabbath's music also exemplifies that culture is continually in music and always in a process of hybridization (Bhabha 1990: 211).

Heavy metal has since been known to reach out to new, cultural forms after settling into a culture after multiple generations. In this regard African nations are very much neophytes to metal and its subculture; simultaneously with most metal fans around the world likely unfamiliar with the scope of the genre's reach within the continent, anything that has come out of Africa has been viewed as a surprise within the metal world. Like Western artists, African rock and metal musicians are writing about their circumstances through the lenses that shape their existence.

Arka'n Asrafokor's invoking of pre-colonial traditions for lyrical themes serves to help local fans be more cognizant of what was once theirs, as well as educating fans from outside of their country about an aspect of their national history that would easily be overlooked. The use of these lyrical themes serves as an empowerment, a reinforcement of identity and a validation of the self, instead of those of an exotic other. Yet, Africans are not viewed in the same light as their Western counterparts.

Hybridization is not viewed or heard equally between acts from the Global South[4] and the Global North, as the contributions of the performers is also left to the bias of the genre's audience and Western-based industry, which has long marginalized African musicians and quietly dictated that Africans perform 'African sounding' music (Scherzinger 2004: 590).

Heavy metal bands, from both the Global North and South, are expressing their music through an interpretation that is comfortable to them, which, as Simon Frith posits, is normal within the world of rock and its various sub-genres that 'can be seen as the authentic articulation of a local identity' (cited in Gligorijevic 2011: 144). Arka'n Asrafokor's association with Togo, or 'African metal' will likely continue to follow them as they gain more awareness in Western markets because every single band that is from the Global South that has embraced elements of their national identity will be linked to their local identity until Westerners can clear their vision of the exotic gaze.

Accessing the Global North

Having been afforded the opportunity to spend time with countless heavy metal bands throughout Africa, it is easier to understand the challenges that metal bands in the continent are facing when it comes to gaining access Western markets – whether it comes from the lack of musical acumen (especially heavy metal), the deleterious conditions that hamper infrastructure or the channels of accessing Western merchandise, notably instruments and recording equipment.

Quick glances throughout Arka'n Asrafokor's rehearsal space gave me the impression of a facility not out of place by Western standards. Situated behind the house that Enrico, Rock and Richard share was a small, inconspicuous room detached from the main residence, flanked by a high wall and an outdoor washroom. Upon entering I stepped up into the sight of a soundboard between two large studio monitors and various pieces of studio equipment on a desk. An air conditioner and sofa behind the desk furnished a room divided by a wall with a sizable plexiglass window that stared directly into a cobalt blue painted space where the band had their equipment set up for their frequent rehearsals and recordings.

With the band rehearsing their setlist (preparing the concert detailed at the outset of this chapter), I noted the instruments they were using; upon closer look, it was nothing I had ever seen before, owing to the circumstances of what was available to them. Bassist Francis laughed slightly when I spoke 'Givson' out loud with a curious look, knowing that what he was playing was a Chinese knockoff intended to fool consumers who wanted an instrument modelled after one of the more iconic names in rock and metal. But this was the best he could do considering his finances. This was Togo after all. Shortly thereafter Rock strapped on his 'Insane' guitar, another Chinese made instrument; this time a six-stringed guitar whose headstock had a font identical to that of the Ibanez guitar company, an instrument manufacturer also synonymous with heavy metal guitarists and bassists. I was curious, however, about the original seven-stringed Jackson guitar – a company that is also highly revered for their instruments among heavy metal guitarists – on which Rock was performing, wondering if there were avenues to access these types of instruments in Togo. He informed me that their manager (who holds a French passport) had travelled to the United States and returned to Togo with this guitar after giving her a list of which guitars he preferred and the money he had saved to purchase the instrument.

Togo is poor. The World Bank's assessment of the nation places more than half of the country as living below the national poverty line, with life expectancy hovering at around 60 years (World Bank 2019: n.pag.). According to the CIA's World Factbook, based on 2017 information, Togo ranks 215 out of 228 in global GDP per capita ratings (CIA 2017: n.pag.).

Poverty is everywhere.[5]

The members of the band are by observed definition middle-class. All of the members are employed, with two of them in possession of their own motorcycles as a form of primary transportation. Yet much of what is seen and experienced in the band's hometown is a facade; things seem beyond reach for everyone who is not connected to the government's ruling party. The country's status quo is one of many hands reaching in unison toward something they will never get. If anyone in Togo wants to experience social and political mobility, any one of the flights to Paris that departs daily is likely the easiest way to do so.

Press watchdog organization Reporters Without Borders (RSF) ranked Togo 76th out of 180 in their 2019 survey citing journalist's apprehensions in discussing political corruption, the military, and the president and his family (RSF 2019). When it comes to entertainment, however, the press take a looser approach, as I witnessed when the French language TV5 Monde (Herman 2019) came to tape Arka'n Asrafokor during one of their rehearsals, as well as their concert.

The band tells me they avoided speaking openly about politics and chose to use their cultural background as lyrical content as opposed to a political stance. As an indication of how apprehensive political discourse can play out in public, Enrico and Rock's father had requested they abstain from discussing politics during our interviews, especially with a foreigner. This was driven by the fear that any information I could potentially publish in a newspaper or magazine article would be read by a government official.

What the band members relayed to me after I established confidence with them over the course of my visit was their frustrations with the life that was in front of them, mostly the realities of Western ambitions that are pulling the Togolese in various directions, confusing pursuits that may never meet expectations. For the members of Arka'n Asrafokor, decolonization is a reclamation of who they are supposed to be in a nation surrounded by a population chasing the West's and France's idea of who they were asked to be, as it was the French who left an imprint on the consciousness of the modern Togolese state.

'For us, the tribes, it's not about fighting against the power, it's about fighting for what is seen among other things', says Rock (2019), noting that the political structure of the nation will remain regardless of who is in charge of the nation because of the strings being pulled by Western powers – the United States, the United Kingdom and France – the nations that the current president serves. It is just the name of the system that has changed. 'Everyone knows that Togo is not ruled by Togolese. It's not, because they just changed the name of the system: Colonialism, corporations. It's bullshit' (Rock 2019: n.pag.).

Conclusion

Arka'n Asrafokor's entrance into the metal dialogue is what the genre needs. The quintet has allowed a non-African, non-Togolese audience to plug into something that is genuinely Togolese. Much in the way that Sepultura showed what is possible in heavy metal, by refining 'what had hitherto been understood as *Brazilian* music' (Avelar 2011: 147, original emphasis), by incorporating a nation and a heritage into an already established and globally familiar sound, Arka'n Asrafokor has built on the template set by reinventing Togo, and reshaping a dialogue around what is possible in heavy metal by performing something beyond 'Togo-metal', or 'African metal'.

The members are quite content with their place in the metal world because it is the only comfort that they know. Togo is home. Africa is home. Ewe culture is their identity. The band's brand of metal is all of these things and the dialogue that heavy metal truly needs.

Yet it remains a standard practice that the most successful acts within heavy metal are primarily based in the West – the Global North. This template of pushing heavy metal into new forms of the reinvented local thought must be equally accepting if Arka'n Asrafokor and other acts from Africa can gain validation from Western audiences. The challenge of heavy metal is that it has never welcomed an all-Black African act to step into the dialogue of the formidable and legitimate; only in modicum do we see members of bands who are Black on Western stages, less so any representation from Africa. The honesty here is that when Arka'n Asrafokor appears on the radar of prospective fans, it is impossible for many to not note their skin colour, likely playing a significant factor into how they will judge their music and their performance (Kotarba and Vannini 2009: 104).

Arka'n Asrafokor's music is not a contradiction of heavy metal or what the genre can be. Their music is a strong representation of hybridization and one that has successfully combined the passions and ambitions of musicians whose aspirations lay beyond their West African frontiers. In doing so, they represent an authentic form of heavy metal, one that sees the genre once again reinvented and reimagined a hybridity that is typical of an 'interconnected world' (Kotarba and Vannini 2009: 137). The band have successfully negotiated and reinforced their Ewe traditions and national identity despite a perception of 'relatively weak' national identities in Africa (Murphy 2007: 43) alongside an already familiar heavy metal template.

What is necessary for Arka'n Asrafokor and other African rock and metal bands who wish to push themselves in the Global North is to understand that their existence is going to be measured by where they are from until their music begins to be seen as its own entity. While African acts do not bear the responsibility of performing to a series of expectations based on stereotypes, 'African societies have been called to reinvent themselves in order to confront the ecological, cultural, political, and social challenges that have emerged' (Sarr 2019: 16–17). Africans today are not attached to a tradition that was theirs to inherit when conflicted with modernity that has failed them.

Arka'n Asrafokor is not only just trying to get through the door that is the barrier to entry in the global metal dialogue, but they are also dead set on breaking the door down so that other African acts can get through, performing the style of heavy metal or hard rock they wish to, whether or not those acts choose to incorporate their local or not.

This is *their* art.

After sitting for an extensive two-hour interview, Rock and I retreated to his living room to relax for a bit and unwind as the sun was setting that Sunday evening. Not long afterwards Rock had asked if he could add something, as there was a thought in his head that he felt he needed to get out. He wanted me to know that their music, to them, was art. This was a reflection of who they were, and how they choose to be seen and heard, and they will be just fine playing the music that best suits them as heavy metal was the only vehicle that many people have to see the rest of the world.

'I think metalheads are already quite open to the world around them. Metal is freedom and an embrace', he says (Rock 2019: n.pag.). Metal for him was not what someone else had constructed for him. It is a response to his life and his surroundings.

His comments harkened back to something similar he said during their concert the previous night. Just before the band played their final song, after already having been in the venue for over twelve hours, Rock stood confident and relieved by what was transpiring in front of him: a receptive audience jubilantly embracing their music, celebrating what was also theirs (see Figure 1.4). He stood quietly for a few seconds catching his breath, sweat beading down his face, with his right hand placed on his hip, left hand clutching the neck of his guitar. Cracking a slight smile, he took a step up to the microphone thanking the crowd in his native Ewe before speaking in English: 'This is our music, for our country, our continent, our Earth'.

FIGURE 1.4: Arka'n Asrafokor after a great performance and one very long day. Photo by the author.

2

Dark Suburb:
The Rebellious Sons of a Nation
and the Amplifying of the Silent in
the City of Hope

The instructions were clear: I could photograph them, but only if the 'skeletons' have their masks on. If I took a photograph of them with their masks off, I would kindly be asked to delete it. The band manager's request was stern. His demeanor, however, indicated that he would not be as callous if the time came. But, I was going to honour his request. The 'skeletons', after all, required anonymity if this was going to work.

The skeletons were a playful nickname for the band Dark Suburb, a masked sextet based in Ghana's capital city, Accra. The rock band first grabbed my attention in 2015 with the release of their first single, 'I Dey Feel You Die' (Dark Suburb 2015), the first rock song I had heard from Ghana.

Dark Suburb had also ventured to Togo as a supporting act for Arka'n Asrafokor. Their patience throughout the nine-hour soundcheck was thinner than mine, so they departed to a nearby hotel before returning several hours later, rested and ready to tune up. They returned for their portion of the soundcheck with a buzz swirling about their presence – six grown humans wearing skeleton masks playing rock music in west Africa was not a common sight (see Figure 2.1). Even a group of children from the neighbourhood came in to sneak a peek at the band during their soundcheck. Everyone was curious.

Dark Suburb is a band redefining expectations. And I wanted to learn more about them. They were never a part of the plan. I had never considered Ghana, or Dark Suburb, when drafting the original ideas for this book. But, after sitting with the band's vocalist, Kankan Bizin, before their soundcheck (which they performed in their masks) and explaining my work and vision for the book that I was sketching out, he, too, shared his vision for what he felt Dark Suburb could be moving forward – a band with a purpose, a 'positive reinforcement for generations'

FIGURE 2.1: The masked skeletons of Ghana, Accra's Dark Suburb in 2019. Photo by the author.

(Kankan Bizin 2019: n.pag.). Beyond the visual aesthetics, Dark Suburb was an extension of Ghana's history and people, an ideal and voice for those who reside deep in their country's forgotten and ignored corners, products of globalization, urban dwellers who were reduced to squalor and are otherwise unheard. Kankan and I agreed to meet again later that evening at the band's hotel.

Rested and unmasked, he informed me I could refer to him by his given name while in his room, reiterating that it was important to keep the character going in the venue for the sake of adding intrigue, to keep people talking. The name Kankan Bizin, he explained, was an amalgamation of 'Kankan', one of the names of Mansa Musa, the great emperor of Mali Empire (see Levtzion 1963) and 'Bizin', who he says was the leader of a *griot* clan of northern Ghana's Dagomba people. This character was important to him, as were all of the characters of the band: guitarists Shamba and Samory Toure, bassist Khama, keyboardist Akhenaten, and drummers Shaka Zulu and Alfanso. 'Our characters are some sort of heroes from African heritage. [Our] villains are poverty, hate, corruption, etc.' (Kankan Bizin 2020: n.pag.).

Anonymity was also important to Kankan Bizin (hereinafter referred to as Kankan), and to the other skeletons who were also unmasked that evening, walking in and out of the room to double-check the scheduled departure time for their performance that night. Kankan requested that I not use his real name because of the sensitivity of the profession he holds in Ghana and the responsibility that comes with his chosen line of work. I have chosen to honour his request of anonymity and to also omit any reference to his profession per that request.

The rebirth of Kankan

Everything that has transpired for Dark Suburb can be traced back to the moment that Kankan met a Western music producer living in Accra in 2010[6] by way of a mutual friend. After hearing him sing, the producer informed Kankan that he should consider forming a rock band in order to perform to his vocal strengths. Unfamiliar with the genre, he went to a local shopping mall in Accra to purchase a CD of a rock band, allowing a catchy cover to dictate his purchase. He settled on Linkin Park's live album *Road to Revolution: Live at Milton Keynes* (2008). The California-based band's music roped him in immediately, and he knew that the next step was to find other musicians with similar interests and form a rock band, which finally happened for him in late 2014. But, it would be important for him, and the rest of the band, to relay a hard rock sound that also informed the listener that they were not just another Western simulacrum alternative rock act, but a band from Accra, Ghana.

An aspiring filmmaker, too, Kankan also felt it would be best to draw a visual concept around his band, one that could also revolve around African history after being told by his grandfather that they were descendants of the great former king of the Malian Empire, Mansa Musa. A thought that had remained with him, regardless of whether it was true or not, was his way of continuing the story of Musa (Kankan Bizin 2019).

Furthermore, Kankan held an interest in his country's masquerade culture and gradually evolved his ideas into the skeletal masks, a detail he felt would be best to pursue:

> The masquerades that came from Africa were there to remind the Kings and the people to be [...] for social progress. So then I worked with the masquerade culture. But what was the mask supposed to represent? That's when I came up with a skeleton mask. If you're dead and you're resurrected as a dead person you're not afraid to tell the truth, because you can't die twice.
>
> (Kankan Bizin 2019: n.pag.)

Disguised as skeletal forms, the members of Dark Suburb portray themselves this way to inform audiences of an anti-racism cause, of the equality that lives beneath the skin where everyone is a skeleton, not a nationality or a skin colour, a language, a religious or ethnic group. The band's song 'Colorblind' (Dark Suburb 2017a) from their 2017 debut full-length album *The Start Looks Like the End* (Dark Suburb 2017d) establishes this identity of promoting 'social justice and tolerance' (Kankan Bizin 2020). Kankan sings in a soft rasp:

> It's much better if we don't see colour,
> Loving one another, that's what matters.
>
> (Dark Suburb 2017a)

Their intentional masking is meant to deflect the individual musician's identity and places audiences into a position of viewing the musicians as the new identities in which they have chosen to present themselves; the change is made more profound when the masks are more 'unnatural, grotesque or frightening, or are abstracted from a human animal figure' (Segy 1976: 2).

Noted for his work with Ebira masquerades of Nigeria, John Picton details that masking, regardless of culture and geography, places the performer into an assumed role for the audience that creates 'a dramatic intention, by effecting distance between performer and audience' (Picton 1990: 191), a transformation that differs from the everyday behaviour of the performer. Yet, as Picton continues, by effecting distance the masks are denying a 'human agency', stating:

> For the masker the separation between everyday self and performed identity is extreme. He is, at the very least, meta re-identified, and in the most extreme cases the mask, in effect, effaces his very existence. The mask, with its costume and accoutrements is the acceptable face, so to speak, of something, a power, an energy, a metaphysical presence, otherwise too dangerous to see. Secrecy will be an essential in a way in which it is not in other cases, for the human agent in performance is no mere animator of a mask, nor is he just an actor in a play. He has entered a space that belongs to and is held to be, in itself, something other.
>
> (1990: 192)

With their identities concealed, Dark Suburb become characters that represent West Africa's past, storytellers in a modern world, keeping a story of the dark suburbs at the forefront of what they are doing.

Dispatches from the edge

When it came to selecting a name for his band, Kankan's decision was simple – find a moniker that could represent the underprivileged, the lives of the many in and around Accra whose existence has long been ignored and overlooked. He sought a name that would speak for the lives of those in the deepest and most desperate clutches of poverty – slums – the dark suburbs.

Slums, or informal settlements, exist because of the ever-increasing costs associated with formal housing. As a result of the illegal, thus informal, nature of these settlements, many residents living in these neighbourhoods do so in incredibly condensed spaces with only a few able to access proper sanitation, fresh water and legal electricity due to many of the residents lacking building permits. As King and Amponsah state: 'These characteristics of slums/informal settlements make them inhabitable and therefore planning authorities by law do not consider such places in urban planning. Consequently, they miss out on having their basic needs met by the state' (2012: 287).

Slum life is the stark reality for far too many around the world, not just in Africa. According to a 2018 UN report, over one billion people worldwide live in slums, with 238 million of those living in slums doing so in Africa (UN-Stats 2018). By 2050, it is expected that 70 per cent of people on earth will be living in a slum (UN-Habitat 2019: v), an increase from the 47 per cent that inhabited slums in 2000 and the 65 per cent who are expected to reside in slums in 2030 (King and Aponsah 2012: 286). Cities of the future will not be lined by glass-stacked skyscrapers with concrete foundations, but rather out of 'crude bricks, recycled plastic, cement blocks, and scrap wood' (Owusu et al. 2008: 180).

These dark suburbs have existed in Ghana for as long as there have been job seekers. The city, which is an amalgamation of British, Dutch and Swedish outposts, saw its profile increase as a trading port in the late 1800s. Known as the Gold Coast while under British rule, the nation stood, like every other colony in Africa, as a business model. Before independence Accra had become an important port for British goods, and, with the Gold Coast one of the treasured colonies of British rule, became the capital in 1877. The prospects of work had made Accra a destination for not only other Ghanaians but also for Africans in neighbouring states.

However, like many colonial possessions in a postwar world, the ruling states were feeling the pressure of independence by way of liberation movements and prominent voices, including 'Africa's Man of Destiny' (James 2017: 267), Kwame Nkrumah, one of the more celebrated figures in the Pan-African movement. The nation's first president and founding father, Nkrumah continues to be revered globally as an icon for his promotion of Pan-Africanism, a belief that all African people, whether on the continent or in the diaspora, share a common destiny as a result of the collective lived experiences of Black people around the world. Or, as Wallace describes it, Pan-Africanism is the 'desire to create a common identity, solidarity, security, and oneness with each other and with Africa' (2014: 71).

When Ghana achieved freedom on 6 March 1957, the nation not only became sub-Sahara's first independent state but also served as the glimmer of light needed for other African leaders who were seeking to shed their colonial chains.

Nkrumah's vision for an independent Ghana was ambitious. His ascendency marked a larger reach and validation for Pan-Africanism and his brand of social-ism, known as 'consciencism'. Publishing his work *Consciencism* in 1964, Nkru-mah outlines a syncretic ideology encompassing indigenous traditions, Islamic socialism and European Christianity, technological and scientific moderniza-tion alongside African unity, a philosophy that is regarded as one of the more 'important doctrines of decolonization' (Ki-Zerbo et al. 1993: 481). A key feature for his vision was centered around socialism for a few reasons. Notably it was, he felt, the fastest way to industrialization in Ghana and a response to the looting of the country by the capitalists of colonialism. His vision of consciencism was embraced by other leaders in Africa, too, including those in Egypt, Guinea, Mali and Tanzania, among others.

Nkrumah's leadership found itself in a polarizing place between Eastern promises and Western ambitions – communism versus capitalism. His presidency was also caught in the conundrum faced by leaders during the independence era that would hit full stride in the 1960s, who were asked to pursue democratic practices while their colonial leaders ruled through authoritarianism and to pursue capitalism while their colonial nations transitioned to socialist welfare states after the Second World War.

The intellectual climate was well suited for socialism in a continent emerging from colonial rule, in part due to the longstanding idea that traditional African cultures were inherently collectivist, practiced shared decision making, held communal lands and maintained networks of social obligations (Meredith 2005: 145). In the eyes of Africans, everyone in a society had to work and play their part. Despite these longstanding collectivist practices, though, 'the sociological and material soil has not proved fertile enough for socialism' (Ki-Zerbo et al. 1993: 486–87).

Ghanaians, too, had given up on Nkrumah. The once-celebrated icon found himself ousted via coup d'état in 1966. Politically, Ghana proceeded through more political unrest as the country experienced three more coups, in 1972, 1979 and 1981, until it was able to find a firm footing. The latter two coups were orchestrated by Jerry Rawlings, a former military leader who would lead Ghana for over 20 years. Rawlings' leadership was tumultuous early on, marked by a totalitarian streak and an economic model that looked towards the Soviet Union. The nation was sliding into failed state status. As Felix Kumah-Abiwu notes, Ghana's post-independent existence was marked by constant 'policy failures, economic mis-management and corruption [...] the Ghanaian economy during the early 1980s was close to a total collapse' (2016: 303). During this period, Accra's population growth slowed with little prospects fueling desires.

Though Rawling's leadership can be remembered for his early tyranny and strong-handed rule, Ghana would likely not have tilted towards responsible economic management and transitional democracy without his eventual shift in policy, abdicating Soviet aspirations for Western models. It was during Rawling's leadership, in the 1990s, that Accra's population accelerated as a result of economic liberalization and greater access to 'global capital' (Owusu 2013: 4). As the nation's 'economy recovered following the adoption of structural adjustment programs (SAPs) and liberalization policies' (Doan and Oduro 2011: 6), Accra's population grew.

According to a 1960 census, Accra's population had increased steadily since the late 1800s to around 370,000 residents shortly after independence (Doan and Oduro 2011: 5). By the year 2000, the population of Accra had grown to 1.6 million, which proved difficult to contain. In a city of 241 square kilometers, Accra's capacity to meet the growing population had met its breaking point, as a spillover of the population had occurred (Twum-Baah cited in Doan and Oduro 2011: 6). With little option, the masses poured into slums. Twenty years later, according to the World Population Review (2020), the population of Ghana's capital city has exceeded 2.5 million, with over half of the city's population estimated to live in any one of the 29 slums dotting the urban landscape (King and Amponsah 2012: 287).

Having been raised in a less than 'slummy' slum himself (Kankan notes that his parents were actually fairly well off compared to many of his neighbours) Kankan continues to make his home in a slum regarded as one of the worst off in Accra, Agbogbloshie. A sprawling slum near Accra's city centre that is home to 40,000 residents, Agbogbloshie is known globally as an electronic waste or e-waste dump (Beaumont 2019; see Figure 2.2). The computer on which I am writing this book could possibly end up there someday, taken apart by kids working without any training in an incredibly hazardous environment and burned so the metallic

FIGURE 2.2: Two men working burning e-waste in Agbogbloshie. Photo by Muntaka Chasant, 2019. Used by permission via Creative Commons.

components bound up in this machine's memory drive, screen and keyboard could be sold for what will likely amount to a derisory wage so the majority of the kids can afford their school fees (Yeebo 2014).

The work done by children will more than likely scar them with health conditions that will plague their adult lives. A 2014 study found that the emissions from the electronics known as polycylic aromatic hydrocarbons (PAHs) led to health problems among many of the study's participants (none of whom were under the age of 18). Participants of the study were more likely to complain 'more frequently about clinical symptoms such as coughs, chest pain and vertigo' (Feldt et al. 2013: 375). The contaminants associated with the burning of electronics could also have a lasting effect on the areas surrounding Agbogbloshie, including the nearby produce markets. The Odaw River that flows around the slum and into Accra's center is not only 'virtually dead' but also likely contaminated with lead (Caravanos et al. 2011: 24) as a result of the excessive pollution and waste that end up in the river (Chama et al. 2014: 1).

On their debut album's second track 'Lunatic Question' (Dark Suburb 2017c), the listener is asked to consider this struggle during the song's second verse:

You are cutting down your trees bringing the desert to your door,
You punch big holes into the ozone with your plenty toys [...]
What kind of world are you leaving for all our growing children?

(Dark Suburb 2017c)

These masked skeletons have embraced their band name to serve as a voice for not only the kids who scavenge this e-waste dump but also for all of the nearly 40 per cent of the Ghanaian population (Index Mundi 2019) who live in slums and are often ignored. The band has chosen to focus their music for a cause that they wholeheartedly believe will change the way the rest of the world views slum dwellers. Thus, they have turned their focus towards helping the residents of Accra-area slums in various ways, including working with local non-government organizations (NGOs) to help further education, skill training and development initiatives, clean water, health, sanitation and entrepreneurship opportunities.

With these intentions, the band hopes that these qualities of life initiatives can serve to improve life for residents in the slum. For example, in August 2020, Kankan had arranged for free health care screenings to be done during the COVID-19 pandemic in Agbogbloshie from health care workers who volunteered their time free of charge to residents (Dark Suburb 2020a). On using Agbogbloshie as a base for their work, Kankan explains that this particular slum is a 'very sad' place that forces you to confront just how brutal poverty is. If Dark Suburb's efforts can work here, he says, they can work anywhere (Kankan Bizin 2020).

This lack of attention to development has likely arisen from the view that slums are viewed by the government as a nuisance. As Oteng-Ababio and Grant state: 'Public officials keen to modernize the booming city often view the poor making a living by sifting through rubbish, or hawking on the streets as a hindrance, and as usurpers of public spaces meant for formal business and wealthy residents' (2020: 357).

Ghana has made progress in attacking poverty and is on track to meet its Millennium Development Goals (MDG Monitor n.d.).[7] Since 1991–92 the country's population living on less than two dollars a day fell from 52 per cent to 28 per cent in 2005–06, while extreme poverty fell from 36.5 per cent to 18.2 during that same period (Yeboah et al. 2015: 259). Today Ghana ranks 74th on World Bank's 2019 GDP assessment, making it a middle-income nation that enjoys a free press and successful democratic institutions. However, as of 2010, as a result of the increasing migration towards this expanding city and 'inadequate infrastructure' (Gaisie et al. 2019: 7), over 'half of the entire population in Ghana live in houses where they have no access to adequate sanitary facilities, water and warmth' (Obeng-Odom and Amedzro 2011: 128). Ghana, like any middle-income nation on the planet, faces the stark reality that something else needs to be done in order to truly help people get out of poverty. The *laissez-faire* approach to wealth building is failing.

For many from Ghana's urban and rural centres, Accra, the 'city of hope' (Awumbila et al. 2014: 17), represents a gateway to possibilities and the rest of the world. The city's profile has increased since the mid 1990s not only as a regional hub but also as a global destination for international companies, government agencies and tourism. Well-constructed roadways connect locals and visitors to any variety of high-end cafes, nightclubs and shopping malls tucked between a modestly sized skyline that hits the eye while standing amid the waste of Agbogbloshie, less than a 20-minute drive from the Parliament building (Yeebo 2014). The cruelty of life in a slum is how close its residents are to the world they aspire to. This is the desperation the band captured well in their 2014 song 'Get Out', one Kankan says highlights the 'evil' of poverty (2020):

You make me a useless family man,
With no resources to my name,
You do not respect any man,
Can't look my children in the face,
They don't get no food to eat,
My baby don't respect me now,

Poverty is all his fault,
Get out of my life ... get out!

(Dark Suburb 2014)

'Get Out' captures the struggles of a man desperate to provide for his family, yet entrenched in a battle against poverty, which has taken on a more animistic form of its own during the song (Kankan Bizin 2019). Further, this song also sees the protagonist confront their identity, one that has been challenged by the seemingly insurmountable task of climbing his family out of their predicament, a struggle that is growing increasingly difficult for anyone living in a slum.

A 2014 survey comparing two slums in Ghana – Nima, a formal settlement and the largest slum in Accra, and the informal Old Fadama (which occupies the same peninsula as Agbogbloshie) – determined that migration to the slums from in and around Ghana seldom leads to a better life for aspiring migrants or their families. 'With poorly paid jobs in the informal sector of the city's economy, many migrants are unable to afford the high housing rental charges' (Awumbila et al. 2014: 33). Furthermore, as it takes someone who lives in a slum to respond to the needs of those living in slums, around 90 per cent of the economy that exists within these spaces is informal (Yeboah et al. 2015: 240).

Like much of what Kankan is working towards, NGOs[8] have also set out to improve the lives of the vulnerable throughout the world through various ways. Kankan admits to having looked down on what NGOs are doing, feeling that many are – in his view – 'scams' (2019). Notably, major NGOs spend a small fortune promoting their causes through media campaigns, mailing circulars and television commercials. Like any business, larger NGOs have CEOs and other salaried employees who work at promoting their company than working through it and have invested in offices all over the world as well as subtle reminders that the NGO is receiving a substantial amount of funds. Kankan, by living directly in the heart of a slum, assures me he sees the ineffectiveness of many NGOs and thus has taken a different approach by working with 'organizations who are doing real effective work in the slums [...] preferably they are people who are locals so that we become engaged with honest and sincere foreigners who have been doing work for years' (Kankan Bizin 2020: n.pag.). But how does being in a rock band change the lives of others?

Performing rock music in a country not associated with this genre and using this music to promote their efforts can be a challenge, however, the band has grown comfortable with several approaches, including writing lyrics about the difficulties of life in slums, filming their music videos in this setting, and by giving the residents of Agbogbloshie – a slum labelled as a 'threat to national security' by a former Accra mayor (Oteng-Ababio and Grant 2020: 357) – a microphone. The latter is through an approach they are sharing on their social media platforms through a mini-documentary series known as the *Slum Chronicles*. They hope that as the band's name spreads, so does their work.

Upon visiting Dark Suburb's Facebook page, one gets a sense that their mission is as important as their music: 'Alternative/Afro Rock band with a slum/deprived people development mission' (Dark Suburb n.d.: n.pag.). As already mentioned, the band has not only centred their lyrics on the lives of slum residents but also has provided them with a voice of their own. Dark Suburb has seen this through to fruition by using their social media pages to promote the aforementioned mini-documentary series called *Slum Chronicles*. These short videos feature Agbogbloshie residents in front of a camera telling their stories. Nothing is scripted, nothing is rehearsed. The intention is to humanize the residents, 'the silent majority', (Kankan Bizin 2020: n.pag.) of a slum that is typically only seen as an e-dump. As Kankan explains:

> *Slum Chronicles* is the capture of the real effects of the projects we are evolving through art and culture, allowing the slums themselves to participate in the story telling [...] Because even the Africans need to know the people living in the slums. The history that we have. So we are just talking to people in the slum about their culture, their history, their experiences in the slum where they believe they can develop as people all together.
>
> (Kankan Bizin 2020: n.pag.)

The hopes are that audiences can humanize the residents of Agbogbloshie. The videos are recorded by local film-makers (the band has helped residents learn how to use the cameras and audio equipment) and are edited by local editors, before being posted on the Dark Suburb Facebook page. The band hopes to eventually record these chronicles in other slums in Ghana and as far away as Nigeria. Kankan hopes that viewers will also better understand the youth of the slums, a demographic typically left out of development goals, and one that their documentary series plans to spotlight, frequently, considering it is mostly youth who are digging through the wasteland of electronic devices. He fears that unless something gets done about this, kids growing up in Agbogbloshie are not going to be exposed to education and opportunity, slipping perhaps into the dark underbelly of drugs and gambling (Kankan Bizin 2020). As he warns in the first verse of the song 'Demons' (Dark Suburb 2017b):

Are your fingers for you?
Or you're a tool but you don't know?

Similarly, in the song's second verse, Kankan continues:

> You have fallen for their bait,
> Now your life will go to waste,
> Then you feel you don't own your life no more.

(Dark Suburb 2017b)

Attempts to redirect efforts to assisting children is just one of the challenges that Kankan sees in ensuring that Dark Suburb's vision is achieved. Other efforts include addressing the lack of entrepreneurship opportunities, scam NGOs, and the notable aspect that a rock band wearing skeletal masks is hoping to make a change in people's lives – a detail that Kankan admits has led to some peculiar conversations (2020).

Kankan insists that rock music has a strong place in modern Ghana for various reasons. Notably, this is the music that can shine a brighter light on issues that are left in the dark, as rock is the musical form of an 'activist. I don't know what to call it, but to be a rock musician is to be extremely expressive' (Kankan Bizin 2019: n.pag.), he adds, 'I feel that all the music has to be bigger than art. It's always been bigger. I keep arguing that *griots* [...] their responsibility was to entertain, educate and inform. And the point of all this is to trigger development' (Kankan Bizin 2020: n.pag.). Motivated by his pursuits of sparking change, with an eye towards the past, Kankan has used music and storytelling in a manner that has invoked one of West Africa's more venerated professions, *griots*.

By invoking the role of *griots*, Kankan shifts Dark Suburb into a place of being able to narrate their cultural history as well as navigate their listeners through the social problems they see afflicting their society. The roles fulfilled by *griots* in West African societies – primarily the nations of Mali, Niger and Senegal – are invaluable as they are the links between the traditional and the modern, the captains of the story through verses that are poetic and musical, while simultaneously informative. *Griots* are oral historians, musicians and praise singers who traditionally perform music on any number of instruments including the *kora*, *ngoni* and *balafon*. They also serve roles in their communities as advisors, diplomats, genealogists, reporters and 'masters of or contributors to a variety of ceremonies' (Hale 1997: 250) including weddings and funerals.

Synonymous with West African culture for over 700 years, the first written descriptions of *griots* have been traced to 1352–53, when the North African traveller Ibn Battuta detailed his introduction with *griots* at the court of Mali (Batoutah cited in Hale 1997: 250). *Griots* continue to remain prominent in West African societies with a social status that, while once having served royalty, today borders on ambiguity. Patricia Tang says because of the *griots* adroit use of the word, whether for veneration or criticism, '*griots* have traditionally held an ambiguous social status, both revered and feared. Because of their right to ask for money and gifts from the people they praise, *griots* are sometimes seen by others as greedy and opportunistic' (2012: 80).

Griots have come to symbolize what is positive about the preservation of African history. Yet, they have also come to mark the romanticism of it as well, with many musicians, poets and writers in and out of Africa often referring to themselves as *griots*. Tang argues that *griots* are often romanticized – and appropriated – because of their reverence and history in the continent, an idea which she describes as static: 'The traditional verbal artist who, for over a millennium, has served as keeper of oral history, musician, singer, and instrumentalist [...] has since become a catchphrase broadly used in reference to modern Africa and African-American artists' (Tang 2012: 81). Thus, the proclivity of modern musicians to associate themselves as *griots*. Tang's description of the idea of *griot* culture being a 'static' one is salient because outside observers of African culture seldom grasp that culture is never in a stasis position; cultures are always in motion, living entities, inhaling and exhaling breath, creating new stories every day. *Griots* continue to carry out valuable orations that link the past and the present and Africans all over the world (Hale 1997: 271) and are not only guardians of their region's history but also keepers of a cherished oral history.

Musicians in West Africa have invoked the role of *griots* as a form of appropriating a deeper place in their history, notably, rappers in Senegal who, like *griots*, feel they, too, are not only masters of the word but also relevant in 'social function' (Appert 2011: 10). This attachment to the *griots* is in part formed by the significance placed on their 'mythos' (Belcher 2004: 172) created by their veneration in West African society.

Damon Sajnani details the way in which rappers in Senegal are using their music to highlight the political norms and the abysmal economic destitution that their leaders have pushed their nation into. Rappers such as Djily Bagdad, Sister Fa and Pacotille are the voices confronting social issues including democratic rights, female genital mutilation and economic uncertainty. Their ways place them alongside *griots* through a practice of using words to voice their 'struggles against injustices' (Sajnani 2013: 171). However, rappers in Senegal, as Sajnani states, have mostly rejected this notion, or 'trope', that they are modern *griots* (2013: 161) precisely because of this commitment to social issues almost exclusively. Their dismissal of this trope is likely out of respect for the profession. But the efforts and reverence of this treasured profession by rappers, much like Kankan, are being utilized by way of their own forms of social activism. And, as a result, are very much performing a similar function to *griots*.

FIGURE 2.3: Dark Suburb performing live in Lomé, Togo in 2019. Photo by the author.

Kankan's intentions are not to fill the role of a *griot* in a traditional sense as much as it is to honour the traditional role of the *griot*, allowing his band's audience to better understand the importance that *griots* served in pre-colonial society, one that has not been lost on the members of Dark Suburb (see Figure 2.3). This is the band's way of negotiating their history with the present, in a manner that does not incorporate local instrumentation to their sound, serving to amplify the voices of those who are otherwise unheard, much like the work of rappers in Senegal (Appert 2016: 243).

The aforementioned examples of rappers in Senegal are worth bringing to light as their work and effort to lend their voices to causes they felt worth pursuing bear comparison to the work that Dark Suburb has undertaken. For Kankan, he understood that among the roles *griots* serve, those of 'ancient African journalists' (2019), is one in which information is relayed down to generations for the benefit of a culture, a preservation of voices and moments that would be passed forward to incoming generations who would recall their ancestors' struggles and wisdom.

Rockin' the highlife

When Kankan recalled his trip to the Accra shopping mall to buy his first rock CD, he had very little knowledge that rock music had once been performed in his country. Much of my experiences throughout Africa have shown me that many believe their generations are the first to embrace rock music in their respective nations. For example, South Africans in the metal scene were not aware that the genre was being performed during the nation's apartheid years; Kenyans of today were not aware that rock music was being performed and recorded in the country decades prior; and Zimbabweans were discreetly aware of the late 1970s 'fuzzy guitar' scene that was also occurring in Zambia. The reality is that Ghana embraced rock decades before Kankan was first exposed to the genre himself, yet there exists a sizable gap in the knowledge and presence of rock music in Ghana.

John Collins, a British-born ethnomusicologist who has been living in and working in the country since the late 1960s, and who has published extensively on Ghanaian music, says that rock 'n' roll found its way into Ghana in the early 1960s by way of imported records and the success of films such as *The Blackboard Jungle* (Brooks 1955) and *Rock Around the Clock* (Sears 1956), which would inspire many 'student and youth bands' including The Avengers, Bachelors and Saints (Collins 2009: 166). The Avengers, formed in 1962, were Ghana's first rock band (Collins 2019: 31). Their arrival inspired more student bands to form, including the aforementioned Bachelors and Saints, as well as Mathew Chapter Five, Blues Syndicate, Circuit Five and the Road Runners, Blue Magic, The Barristers and El Pollos.

These early bands were confronted with conflicting circumstances in their newly independent state – the hope of prosperity and the contemptuous leadership of Nkrumah. During the period of rock music's genesis, Ghana was already in a strong position economically with a reserve of 200 million British Pounds (James 2017: 268). As historian Martin Meredith notes, the country was liberated with an incredible amount of progress:

> Ghana embarked on independence as one of the richest tropical countries in the world, with an efficient civil service, an impartial judiciary and a prosperous middle class. Its parliament was well-established, with able politicians in both government and opposition.
>
> (2005: 27)

However, Nkrumah's leadership was more difficult than would have been assumed at independence. His presidency was notably marked by his paranoid leadership style, which saw him rule by decree, arresting political opponents while pursuing his critics and the press, and controlling the national radio and television. A 1965 profile of him in *The New York Times Magazine* notes that he was obsessed with his work, putting in nearly 20 hours a day because of his reluctance to trust anyone else with the work of running the government (Sale 1965: 38), further describing him as a man obsessed with an ideology without having a sense of the reality that surrounded him (1965: 41). And, he controlled the ability to pull songs from radio at will (Collins 2006: 179). Rock music, however, was largely away from peering eyes.

These early acts primarily focused their performances around a variety of songs by the chart-toppers of the day, including The Beatles and the Rolling Stones. It was during the latter portion of the decade, the post-Nkrumah era, that musicians took a radically different approach, as the era of psychedelic rock ushered in new acts such as the Magic Aliens – sometimes referred to as the Psychedelic Aliens – who took their cues from the sounds of two of the eras dominant acts, Jimi Hendrix and Cream (Collins 2019: 31).

Western hitmakers who also helped to plant seeds of influence include Chubby Checker, who toured the country in 1966 and 1967. Rock 'n' roll had gained enough validation in Ghana that the country, alongside Nigeria, would also become a hot spot for international artists looking for something new and 'exotic'. Guitar legend Santana also performed in Ghana in 1971 for the nation's *Soul to Soul* (Sanders 1971) concert, receiving a visit from drummer Ginger Baker of the famed rock trio Cream who famously documented his visit to the country in the 1970s in *Ginger Baker in Africa* (Palmer 1973). Another Western drummer, Mick Fleetwood of the hugely successful Fleetwood Mac, would also record his 1981 album *The Visitor* in Ghana (see Fleetwood and Shapiro 1981). Ghana may have been an exotic, 'other' location for professional Western musicians stuck in the routine of touring the Global North. But for aspiring musicians in West Africa, this was the validation they had been looking for.

These new sounds that worked their way into Ghanaian music during this era were also influenced by another style of music that likely made rock 'n' roll possible: highlife.

The roots of highlife are long in the making: non-Ghanaian influences worked their way through local music with the advent of European traders in the late 1400s, introducing fife and brass bands, 'sea-shanties of seaman' (performed on harmonicas, guitars, concertinas, accordions and banjos) and later piano-led hymns by Christian missionaries (Collins 1996: xii). Because of this:

> Highlife emerged as three distinct streams, each dependent on which particular western musical influence was assimilated and utilized by the African musicians who fused it with their own tradition. First there was the imported influences of foreign sailors that became 'palm-wine' highlife; second, that of the colonial military brass-bands that became *adaha* highlife; and third, that of the christianized black elite which became dance-band highlife.
>
> (Collins 1989: 222, original emphasis)

By the 1920s, highlife musicians were also incorporating other imported influences, 'such as the Foxtrot and Calypso [likely a result of the West Indian soldiers that were stationed in the country in the late 1800s] into Ghanaian rhythms like *osibisaba*, a guitar and accordion-driven style of music of the coastal Fante population, and a guitar style from Liberia[9] *dagomba*' (Salm and Falola 2002: 181). While colonial rulers had found some of the brass and guitar music of the early 1900s to be 'objectionable', associating the form of dance that accompanied the music as a form of 'social protest' and thereby arresting[10] some of its participants (Collins 2006: 173), Ghanians had found a true musical identity to call their own. Yet for Kankan, when asked about highlife and how it has shaped his musical identity, he felt otherwise. Instead, he felt that this style of music was not truly Ghanaian, but was a vestige of an era where colonial chicanery left its subjects yearning for validation. 'I think what the British left on Ghana was highlife. Even the word is not a genre, it was an elitist word for the high society people. It's not even original', he says (2019). To him, Ghanaians during the colonial rule were desperate for something that could make them feel more British, an aspirational part of a whole that was beyond their reach by design. Highlife was meant to distract Ghanaians from the knavery of colonial rule, where rock music represents what Ghana has actually become.

Highlife was performed by big-band orchestras in clubs frequented by the elite colonial population and Black elites in Accra who would accompany the music with the dances of the foxtrot and the waltz, only later to see these dances absorb more African influences. The term highlife came by way of those who stood outside these exclusive nightclubs, such as the Merry Villas and Palladium Cinemas (Collins 1989: 225), watching the well-dressed pay high entrance fees to watch local musicians perform a local style of music.

Highlife also became a tool of persuasion by performers and political leaders alike. Nkrumah specifically utilized popular music, including highlife, to court political favour through artists' support for his national causes. However, a few highlife artists, such as Bob Cole and E.T. Mensah, found themselves at odds with Nkrumah because their music was critical of his politics and ultimately found their songs pulled from national broadcasts that were being monitored for subversive and indecent content. Thus, to skirt censors, musicians would often mask their messages through parables and allusions (Collins 2006: 178). Censorship in Ghana continued well after Nkrumah was forced from power; the country would not have privately held airwaves until the 1990s (Collins 2006: 179).

In the coming decades, highlife would also be enjoyed outside of West Africa. Formed in London, England in 1969, Osibisa, performed a hybrid style of rock-influenced music, which, alongside highlife, created a genre called 'Afro-rock'. As Collins explains:

> The group, originally called the Cats Paw, played rock music for British dance fans in the late 1960s, but noticed that these youths enjoyed the Africanized rock songs

the group occasionally played [...] so the band decided to focus on this music. They renamed the group 'Osibisa', led by the Ghanaians Teddy Osei, Mac Tontoh and Sol Amarfio, who had previously all been dance band highlife musicians. Indeed, the band's name is derived from the old Akan name for highlife, *osibisaaba* – and some of Osibisa's songs such as 'Music for Gong Gong', [1971] were based on highlife rhythms. Over a 20-year period from 1970 on this band toured all over the world and released dozens of top-selling records.

(Collins 2019: 31: original emphasis)

Early visits by well-known Western musicians served to validate the Ghanaian rock scene, however, with the exception of Osibisa, none of the early bands experienced success outside of West Africa. While the band, which also featured members from the British Caribbean (Salm and Falola 2002: 185), had a strong influence on others in the country to perform this style of music – Afro-rock – they were never based in Ghana at any point during their career.

The band's success, however, assisted in validating rock in Ghana. During subsequent decades, however, rock music did not disappear from the national consciousness as much as it disappeared from the national conversation. Dark Suburb has Ghanaians once again talking about rock music, amongst a generation who had no idea that their country had made a significant contribution to the rock music world.

Ghana's political situation would change course under the leadership of Jerry Rawlings, who eventually began looking to the West for economic stability and, in a decision that caught observers and Ghanians for a surprise, 'Rawlings announced in May of 1991 that Ghana would adopt a multi-party, constitutional, liberal democracy' (Crook 1999: 119). He would subsequently win the country's first two free elections and serve as president until 2001, abdicating his position to the will of the constitution and voters.

Dark Suburb's entrance into Ghana's musical dialogue comes during political and economic circumstances that are unlike any that their predecessors were confronted with. Today's version of the country is often celebrated as one of Africa's success stories for the notable reason that it has seen a double turnover of opposing political parties by way of elections for decades, a feat that has been accomplished in only five African countries. Ghana's political system is defined by its 'well-institutionalized party systems' where political ideology and not identity lead party leaders to believe in a system of democratic values, not the cynicism of knowing that a loss in an election means a complete and rigid structural national change (Lodge 2013: 24). Most importantly, artists today are not subjected to the censorship that existed in the years leading up to and following independence.

Conclusion

2020 was a year full of uncertainty for many around the world. The arrival of a global pandemic shut down entire economies and the perpetual motion of bodies that travel for pleasure, necessity or work. 2020 was the year the world stood still. As I write this, the toll of the COVID-19 shutdown on various facets of human life, mental health, economic and political systems, as well as the impact the global shutdowns had on our climate, remains to be seen. For Ghana, the pandemic response was one that mirrored its global counterparts by sealing its borders and restricting the movement of its citizens both in and outside of the nation. The impact of the COVID-19 shutdowns, however, will be felt more so in the slums. With what would amount to an economy that barely scratches the surface of formality taking a hit, billions will pay the price. Social distancing in slums is nearly impossible, as was the ability to provide everyone with masks. COVID-19 exposed global economic disparities in a way that nothing, not even willful ignorance, could prevent.

This also meant that my scheduled trip to the country was not going to happen. There would be no Dark Suburb concert in their hometown for me. There would also be no visit to Agbogbloshie as was scheduled. My follow-up interview with Kankan had to occur via a patchy internet connection.

Provided ample time to focus their energy on new music and their projects, there was an underlying blessing through this chaos for the members of Dark Suburb. Kankan used this moment to pursue health initiatives and awareness of the severity of COVID-19. 'If poor people are helpless in the world today, things like this just come to expose what they're really exposed to', says Kankan (2020).

Further, the band of masked performers was also able to focus on reaching out to a larger national audience during a year that saw everyone (well, nearly everyone) masking up! Using their ever-increasing internet presence, Dark Suburb started live streaming acoustic concerts from their rehearsal space, partook in an Accra arts festival, *Chale Wote* via live stream (Dark Suburb 2020b) in late August, while releasing several new music videos, including one that shined a light on an NGO that helps kids in Agbogbloshie enroll into better schools. The band never slowed down.

If 2020 taught musicians anything, especially in Africa, it is that you do not need to focus your interests globally in order to reach new audiences and to hone your craft. Salm and Falola have argued that musical trends during the years immediately following independence indicated the need for Ghanaian musicians to develop their talents and name outside of Ghana (2002: 185). The need to do this now, in a setting that has increasingly shrunk through the process of globalization, seems unnecessary provided the ever-increasing global connectivities.

But for a band on a mission, a global shutdown may have been what they needed to highlight the ever-growing economic disparities all over the world.

This is why what Dark Suburb is doing matters so much to Kankan and the other skeletons; they are quite aware they can make a difference. The events of 2020 are why Kankan has long viewed his role as a musician as one with a purpose. 'It's the responsibility of the musician to push for social change. Because music is a powerful thing and a powerful tool. It's a tool that people listen to; it wakes people up', he says (Kankan Bizin 2019: n.pag.).

Rock and metal's appeal to the marginalized is what has validated these genres' global expansions for generations now. Yet seldom does a band step out explicitly on behalf of the marginalized. At the time of this writing, the only other band known to have come from a slum is Cambodia's Doch Chkae (Wright 2019). Dark Suburb's place in Ghana is special as they are the only one in the country, and likely the continent, to have come from a slum. Africans have long battled for their voices to be recognized and heard, yet it is only a few whose shouts can cut through the crowd of voices heard globally. Perhaps their vision can also serve to empower rock and metal acts elsewhere to follow suit and pursue their own roles in music activism that is unlike any other.

Before Kankan and I cut our interview so he could get ready to make his Togo debut, I asked him if he felt that Westerners would see what he was doing as a vestige of colonialism. Finalizing his wardrobe for the evening, reaching for his mask as we ran to the van to take us back to the venue, Kankan once again emphatically stated that rock music was not something he felt that the British, or any colonial government, could have left behind. For him, this music was too clever to have been left behind by a government set on controlling and extraction.

Looking around the van, the rest of the members slipped into their masks as we were fast approaching the venue, nodding their heads collectively with the feeling that tonight's show was going to be one to remember. The self-proclaimed 'rebellious sons of a nation', (Kankan Bizin 2019: n.pag.; see Figure 2.4) fearless and confident, stared back at me just as Kankan was set to step out of the van. Holding my gaze Kankan added: 'Rock music has the responsibility of speaking the truth, and there's no other perfect genre to do what we're doing than rock music' (2019).

As their manager shut the van door behind me, the members strapped their guitar bags over their shoulders and walked slowly into the venue towards the stage, past the eager audience who were just as curious at who was behind the masks. And with the crowd's energy now focused on the stage, Kankan introduced the band just as the first notes were being strummed.

It was showtime!

FIGURE 2.4: The rebellious sons of two nations – Ghana's Dark Suburb and Togo's Arka'n Asrafokor after a shared performance in 2019 in Lomé, Togo, which included a nine-hour soundcheck. Photo by the author (who finally got to eat, along with the members of these two bands, shortly after this photo was taken).

3

Lights, Camera, Leather!
Kalahari Snapshots, Global Visions and
Marginal Existences

On 2 July 2012, the global media giant CNN travelled to Botswana to meet and interview South African photographer Frank Marshall for a feature on the network's *Inside Africa* program (Barnett 2012a; Barnett 2012b). The reserved, timid Marshall, wearing a faded, oversized military jacket and faded blue jeans, sat at a wooden picnic table outside of the Bee 6 Bar in Gaborone, opposite *Inside Africa's* loquacious presenter Errol Barnett. The two sat to discuss Marshall's photography set, titled *Visions of Renegades* (Kahn-Harris 2011), that highlighted the nation's metal fandom, as well as what Barnett assumed to be the neophyte heavy metal scene in Botswana. Though the interview was arranged beforehand, Barnett walked into the bar to meet Marshall after his 'drive' from an intersection situated just outside of the capital city that introduced the segment.

The segment that opens the piece rolls right into a cliched hyperbole of southern Africa. Barnett highlights the fate of Botswana's beleaguered neighbours – Namibia, Angola and Zambia – explaining to the viewers which European nations had colonized each of those three nations (Barnett 2012a) – but not Botswana, the country he is standing in. Barnett explains that the nation was not a colony but a protectorate, not only drawing a correlation between the nation's political and economic successes but also detailing that because of this history, the nation's population maintains a different mood towards foreigners: 'You could argue the result of that is that Africans here harbor less animosity toward Europeans', he says (Barnett 2012a: n.pag.).

Physically pointing south to South Africa and explaining a bit about that country's tortured history with racism during the apartheid-era, Barnett counters, 'people here have always been able to integrate freely'[11] (2012a). Directing his attention east, towards Zimbabwe, Barnett mentions the disparity between their respective diamond industries, neglecting to state that Zimbabwe's then dictator, Robert Mugabe, had used his county's mine revenues for personal and political benefit.

The introduction by Barnett for his segment on Botswana's metal scene was perhaps his way of trying to understand why there was a metal scene in sparsely populated, landlocked Botswana in the first place. This segment introduction was also a tacit refrain that highlighted heavy metal as a 'White' music, finding it peculiar that the sounds of heavy metal as well as its imagery have managed to find a home in a 'Black' African nation.

The interests in Botswana-based bands grew substantially around the world after images of fans from the nation were published in newspapers and by major media outlets in the early 2010s. It is a reality that fans and musicians in the country are quite aware of – the Botswana metal scene is the most documented and recognizable in the African continent. But why and how did this happen? What is it about this particular scene that has landed the gazes of the curious and into the conversations of Westerners?

This chapter will discuss this interest in the Botswana heavy metal scene from Western media outlets and why this attention has not happened elsewhere in other African scenes. Using examples of published photographs as well as interviews with a few of the photographers themselves, I will highlight examples that support what I feel has potentially led to the gazes from Western fans into this metal scene: othering. Does othering keep the Botswana metal scene in a box riddled with the expectations that a White Global North has constructed for Africa? Or has othering helped the genre gain viability in not only Botswana, but the African continent as a whole?

Barnett was also confused about the genre, likely because he, like so many who do not listen to metal, was not aware that the genre was also well cemented in other African states. What Barnett was doing was 'othering' Botswana, an approach that entails highlighting differences between what is stereotypically expected versus what is actually experienced. By explaining that Botswana was 'not like the others' in the region, he speculates that perhaps this is why heavy metal had found a home here – the reason a 'White' form of music landed in a 'Black' African nation. Barnett, who covered Africa rather well as a journalist, most likely never imagined himself presenting a story on heavy metal scenes. His resorting to labelling genres as identifiers of skin colours is a poor assumption that is not new to the metal world. The idea of associating music with races – which will also be discussed in this chapter – is where much of this discourse begins: who gets to perform what style of music, and who gets to decide what it looks like?

Nosey roads and metal horizons

Barnett began his conversation with Frank Marshall by asking: 'Why is Botswana a good place for metalheads?' (Barnett 2012a: n.pag.). Marshall's response was anecdotal, insisting that the genre has existed in a positive setting in the country for a while by explaining that heavy metal and its hard rock cousin was not a recent embrace by Batswana.[12] Marshall continued: 'I think there's potential for that subculture to exist anywhere. It just needs the right catalyst to set it off. In the research I've done, metal was seeded here by a classic rock band here in the 1970s' (Barnett 2012a: n.pag.).

Rock and heavy metal had an organic genesis in Botswana. The first rock band in the country, Nosey Road, which formed in 1974 as a school band, would become the first group in Botswana to release an album outside of the country with 1983's *Freeway*. Formed by two brothers, bassist Ivo and guitarist Renato Sbrana, their music was influenced by the Western rock stars the two enjoyed, notably Jimi Hendrix. Rounded out by Delia Sbrana (Ivo's wife) on keyboards and drummer Joe Mothum, Nosey Road performed throughout Botswana as often as they could, playing in towns large and small, gaining a substantial fanbase over the years. Their performances were vibrant and known to have drawn great audiences. Their music would serve as a major influence for aspiring musicians in the years to come. Nosey Road were not only the first original rock band in Botswana, but also one of the very first in southern Africa.

Among those influenced by Nosey Road's music was Metal Orizon, a group of aspiring musicians in Francistown, Botswana's the second largest city. Forming in the early 1990s, the band met while attending school together, bonding over their enjoyment of electric guitar-driven music. Their sound marked a departure from the work of Nosey Road, as it was more distorted and their vocal approach, while clean throated, pushed through with more aggression. Metal Orizon is regarded within Botswana as the country's first heavy metal band. Releasing their first album, *Ancestral Blessing* (1999), the band gained a local following that grew by word of mouth and culminated with a national hit song, 'We Are Rolling', off of their *Myopic Enslavement* (Metal Orizon 2001) album. The band's influence made an impression that allowed others in Botswana to follow through with their ambitions as there was now a vision of what was possible in performing and recording original hard rock and heavy metal music. When conducting fieldwork, I often would ask members of other bands and fans which act they viewed as the 'Black Sabbath' of Botswana – the band that every metal musician in the nation could point to as being the one that cleared the road for others to exist. The responses were always without hesitations: Metal Orizon.

With two established acts, the late 90s in Botswana saw other musicians form bands that were able to take their music beyond the borders of Botswana and eventually outside of the continent. Bands such as Crackdust, Wrust, STANE, Amok, Remuda and Skinflint stepped forward alongside Overthrust during the new millennium with markedly more aggressive approaches as their sounds were influenced by a more-diverse intake of Western heavy metal, including death metal, power metal and groove metal. Musicians of this post-90s wave have cited their influences of seminal Western bands such as Manowar, W.A.S.P., Cannibal Corpse, Slipknot, Sepultura, Metallica, Megadeth, Pantera, Trivium, Morbid Angel and Iron Maiden.

This wave of musicians was not only able to use the internet to access their favourite heavy metal records from Western markets but they were also able to use the online infrastructure to promote their bands and music to Western audiences and neighbouring markets, including South Africa and Namibia. Botswana's heavy metal scene, by the turn of the century and in the space of ten years, went from local to global.

One band that blossomed during this era was Wrust, a groove metal trio based in Gaborone. They aggressively took advantage of their proximity to the unfolding metal scene in Johannesburg, South Africa, to become a steady fixture in that nation as well – a privilege that afforded them the opportunity to serve as support for international touring acts including Sweden's Entombed and Brazil's Sepultura following the release Wrust's 2007 debut, *Soulless Machine*. The band's popularity within South Africa grew to the point where many fans in the nation (from personal experience) thought Wrust were a South African band! Wrust were even the subject of a documentary, *March of the Gods: Botswana Metalheads* (Mosca 2014), which culminated in their first tour outside of Africa and a co-headlining slot at the *Solo Macello* festival in Italy.

Similarly Skinflint, another trio based in the Botswana capital, has also taken their sound beyond the dusty landscape of the Kalahari as they too have performed in South Africa, Kenya and Sweden, and in the United States touring as a support band for the Brazilian-American band Soulfly in 2019 and 2020. Since their formation, Skinflint have released six full-length albums, including the first by a Botswana metal band on a Western label, *Skinflint* (2018), on United Kingdom's Into Records.

Through the late twenty-teens, the Botswana scene continued to expand, with bands such as Evergreen, Dust n Fire, Alive n Bolder and Raven In Flesh, building on the work of their predecessors. As this chapter will discuss, the Botswana heavy metal scene is no longer obscure as the bands performing today are well aware of the potential opportunities of their music travelling well beyond their nation. Bands are also very aware of the possibility that performing music at a professional level is viable, though perhaps still very slim.

It was appropriate that Barnett approached Marshall as the introductory interviewee, as the focus on Botswana's heavy metal fan culture began with Frank Marshall. Since his photographs first appeared, there have been at least nine other photographers who have placed Batswana heavy metal fans as their centrepieces (Tamagni 2013; Shiakallis 2015b; Wehelie 2016; Mechanic and

Bonet 2017; Chukura and Rolinec 2017; Brincat 2018; Mmonatau 2014; Jason and Wilbekin 2019; Ciolfi 2019; Todisco 2020), publishing similar photosets. However, it was Marshall's *Visions of Renegades* publication on *Vice* (Kahn-Harris 2011a; see also BBC 2013) that commenced the curiosity. The accompanying article was also the first to be published with a wide circulation that documented an African heavy metal scene. The article commences:

> Love it or hate it, when most people think of metal, they think of white dudes. Even if metal was born from the blues and there are growing scenes in places like Indonesia and Peru, metal's founding fathers – Priest, Sabbath, Maiden – and most of those who've come after them have been unmistakably Caucasian.
>
> (Kahn-Harris 2011a: n.pag.)

Until these publications, heavy metal's image of its performers and fans has been primarily White, male and Western-dominated. Scholar and writer Keith Kahn-Harris – who wrote the article without actually visiting the nation – expresses his surprise in discovering that there was a group of metal fans in a predominantly Black African country who 'knew who Lemmy was' (2011a: n.pag.), referring to the iconic vocalist and bass player of the highly influential British band Motör-head. Kahn-Harris' reference to Motörhead also places the imagery of their most iconic album, *Ace of Spades* (1980), into the conversation as the album's cover features the band standing on a sand dune in a desert, draped in leather, adorned in cowboy boots and hats. Whether or not this served as the cue for fans in Botswana is unknown, as members of the scene have never fully acknowledged this coincidence. The resemblances, however, are uncanny.

Marshall's first intake of the Botswana metal scene came during his first trip to the country when he accompanied a friend's band, Rhutz, from South Africa in 2008 for a performance. It was when the band arrived at the venue that Marshall took notice of the fans waiting outside. His introduction to the MaRock[13] scene left an immediate impression. 'It felt like I had stepped into a fictional world, and there was a magical quality to it all' (Marshall 2019: n.pag.). This was different from the metal subculture he was already familiar within South Africa. Marshall was also taken by the manner in which the fans in Botswana identified themselves, using monikers such as Trooper, Dead Demon Rider, Coffin-feeder and Ishmael Phantom Lord, which allows the fans to detach themselves from their lives outside of the leather, and invoke a different set of rules under a new aegis, much like another notable Western metal scene, the Norwegian black metal scene (Phillipov 2012: 153). Participants in the Norwegian scene have also taken to adapting monikers such as Euronymous, Abbath, Gaahl and Necrobutcher, among others. This practice of adopting pseudonyms, whether in

Norway or Botswana, is a continuation of practice in the metal subculture that has lionized many musicians including Corpsegrinder, Blackie Lawless, Alice Cooper and Marylin Manson.

Already a long-time metal fan and a fixture in the South African metal scene as a live photographer, Marshall's first visit to Botswana was propitious as he was enrolled in a photography program at a Pretoria university when he first visited Botswana. For Marshall, whose degree required a research project for graduation, the tight-knit Botswana metal scene proved to be a good fit. He returned shortly after his first trip with the intention of documenting the fans he met:

> I was interested in the scene [...] from a visual perspective, and I sort of approached the story with a gonzo mentality. I immersed myself in the scene over a period of about eighteen months. Over this time I would attend shows, travel with fans, eat with them, end up at police stations with them when they got busted for carrying weapons [for show] etc. Most importantly, I'm a metalhead myself, and so I viewed the scene as a fan of metal and not simply an outside observer.
>
> (Marshall 2019: n.pag.)

Marshall's images captured fans revelling in a genre that has long been misunderstood and unvalidated by the world of mainstream music. These photos were raw as much as they were natural: emotive snapshots of a metal subculture that few in the world had known existed (see Figure 3.1 and Figure 3.2). In every photograph published, fans not only were seen wearing T-shirts of their favourite metal bands but also were captured in leather, whether it was a jacket, pants, cowboy hat or all of the above. Some of the fans held props such as chains, crosses, spikes or cattle skulls, with a few adorned in spikes. It is part cowboy, part apocalyptic and one hundred per cent Botswana. The attire was influenced by Batswana culture, by their cattle-raising history and by a heavy influence of American western/action films (Vulture 2020: n.pag.) that were popular in Botswana. 'It's cultural, it's natural. It's something we got from our forefathers, our parents, when we were boys herding cattle. Also, we would watch cowboy movies and try to relate that to our lives', says well-known Botswana metal fan Gunsmoke (Metropolis 2013: n.pag.).

A lot of the attention, however, was placed on the fans' leather attire, less on their fandom. And, Marshall, too, acknowledges that a lot of his focus was on the leather attire of the fans. Of the fans he photographed, Marshall told CNN that he felt their style was mostly based on the influence of the New Wave of British Heavy Metal scene from the 1970s:

> We are talking about Iron Maiden, Judas Priest; they very much epitomized that style of leather and spikes and things like that. In my view that's the most aggressive image

FIGURE 3.1: *Trooper* from Frank Marshall's 2011 *Visions of Renegades* series. Photo by Frank Marshall.

FIGURE 3.2: *Bound by the Moon* from 2011 *Visions of Renegades* series. Photo by Frank Marshall.

of metal that's ever existed. It doesn't really exist today in the West. Guys just wear hoodies, sneakers, metal shirts, but they don't go over and beyond like these guys do.

(Barnett 2012a: n.pag.)

Marshall's admission here is honest. Though he alludes to the fact that the Botswana scene was truly 'counterculture' (Marshall 2012: 67), his indications were that there was a notable difference in Gaborone metal scene from what he was used to seeing in his local metal scene of Pretoria and Johannesburg, South Africa – a scene dominated by the nation's White minority.

Visions of Renegades made an immediate impression on those who saw the exhibition. Marshall's images reflected fans in a metal scene unlike any previously seen before. This was a brand new image of metal fans – a new frontier of metal fandom that had yet to be crossed. These images had movement. These were fans living their lives as metal fans their own way, in their own tucked-away corner of the Kalahari desert, and in a manner that identified them as fans of metal, distinguished from other individuals and groups and communities in Western settings (Kruse 1993: 38). These were the 'metal cowboys of Botswana'.

The images of MaRock were seen globally once the original *Vice* article landed on the internet, quickly making an impression among those who saw them. It would not take long before countless simulacrums followed, broadcasting their versions of the same scene, even using the same fans in some instances. Exhibitions by other photographers, including Daniele Tamagni (Tamagni 2013), Aldo Brincat (Brincat 2018; Mmonatau 2014), Paul Shiakallis (Shiakallis 2015a, 2015b; Kelly 2018: 70–72), Pep Bonet (Wehelie 2016; Mechanic and Bonet 2017), Petra Rolinec (Chukura and Rolinec 2017), Lee-Roy Jason (Jason and Wilbekin 2019), Andre Badenhorst (Ciolfi 2019) and Arianna Todisco (Todisco 2020) spilled into galleries and various publications in the years that followed. But what is it about these images that allowed the interest in the subject to remain relevant?

This flocking from the other photographers shifted the talking points as to how the subjects of the photographs, originally captured by Frank Marshall, would be viewed. The Batswana metal fans depicted in the subsequent photographs are being showcased in a manner that lends itself to othering. This is a manner that views non-Westerners through Western gazes instead of understanding or acknowledging the lived experiences of the individuals in question. Othering also reinforces the idea that non-Westerners – '*they*' – are not like us. As Bill McGrath states: 'Focusing solely on the scene's fashion risks presenting the Metalheads as an exotic Other, an African novelty act' (2015: 215). Is McGrath correct? Are Western audiences viewing these metal fans as a novelty act?

The concept of othering stems from European curiosities of identifying and labelling those not like 'us' (Europeans/Westerners) in terms of philosophies, education, religion, arts, literature and customs as different and in some ways inferior to European standards. These curiosities are what led explorers to visit the lands east of Europe as well as Africa. Upon returning to their native countries, travellers would publish their diaries relaying experiences to readers who were crafting assumptions of the citizenry in corners of the world that most would never have imagined of existing. This was othering, as this one-way dialogue was a form of controlling how Westerners viewed humans in seldom visited lands. Mapping humans without a sense of who they were, without discovering their history or studying their ways, was not only lazy but also horrendously ethnocentric. This is what othering created: 'they, them, *those* people'. Othering happened not only because of this creation of an exotic, almost beastly human experience but also because the expectations created by Westerners of others in their mind were not met. Othering occurs today for the same reasons, because 'they, them, *those* people' are not meeting the expectations that Westerners hold about how the rest of the world lives, especially Black Africa. In the realm of Botswana's heavy metal scene, this is what is happening: Western ideas of what is expected from heavy metal culture and from an African country are not being met.

This form of ostracizing empowered Europe before and during the colonial era and still continues. Edward Said, in his seminal work on the subject *Orientalism* (1994), describes the lands away from the European continent where the West has constructed its images of the 'Other', as the West is the 'source of its civilizations and languages, its cultural contestant, and one of its deepest and most recurring images of the Other' (Said 1994: 1). When discussing his philosophy of othering, Said says:

> The construction of identity – for identity, whether of Orient or Occident, France or Britain, while obviously a repository of distinct collective experiences, is finally a construction in my opinion – involves the construction of opposites and 'others' whose actuality is always subject to the continuous interpretation and re-interpretation of their differences from 'us'. Each age and society re-creates its 'Others'. Far from a static thinking, then identity of self or of 'other' is a much worked-over historical, social, intellectual, and political process that takes a place as a contest involving individuals and institutions in all societies [...] In short, the construction of identity is bound up with the disposition of power and powerlessness in each society, and is therefore anything but mere academic woolgathering.

> (1994: 332)

As Staszak writes: 'The creation of an otherness [othering] consists of applying a principle that allows individuals to be classified into two hierarchical groups: them and us' (2008: 2). This concept is not only a result of ethnocentric biases but also Western concepts of exoticism which stem from colonialism. These were the curiosities that guided missionaries, travellers and scholars into Africa and dictated so much of the way that the West would understand how those in the 'other' places would be seen and viewed. What guides Western viewers to see Africa the way they are now is very much a vestige of what was created by preceding generations.

Consider the work of photographer Pep Bonet, whose photo set of MaRock entitled *The Hellbangers* has been published by CNN (Wehelie 2016) and *Mother Jones* (Mechanic and Bonet 2017) as well as in the German magazines *Der Spiegel* (Löwe 2016) and *Die Stern* (Ritter 2017: 74). When interviewed by CNN, Bonet confesses:

> A lot of people think rock 'n' roll is a white man thing, and I'm thinking no way. I think it's black and white and anything in between [...] They have a naivety, or an innocence, which a lot of the bands in America, for example, or in Europe, have lost. Every band resembles another band. If you hear the metal from Botswana, it doesn't look or sound like any other band, and that is, for me, very, very special.
>
> (Wehelie 2016: n.pag.)

Bonet's concession is an honest one, which is what likely is driving much of the attention of the work of the photographers: namely, that metal has long been viewed as a 'White' genre and the arrival of Batswana into the discourse of heavy metal's sacred subculture merits attention. Bonet is relaying a Western construction of viewing the other as a novelty by stating that bands in the West are the mold for what the metal world aspires to, though they are in effect mimicking each other. Yet, Batswana metal bands (Bonet does not mention bands by name) do not resemble Western acts because of this appearance, alluding to the notable differences of skin colour. While his assessment here may be an 'innocuous cultural signifier' (Gallagher 2003: 5) the dialogue of expectations based on racial stereotypes and of societal constructions based on race are salient. Jason Rodriguez says there is a difficulty in managing how an individual from a Western setting may view a culture that is different from theirs (Rodriguez 2006: 646). And as is the case with African existences, othering is validated, because so much of what Africans do is placed into racial context, especially in music.

Though the other photographers[14] had various introductions to the Botswana heavy metal scene, it appears that their motivations were similar. They were intrigued by the distinctiveness of what they encountered (Marshall 2019; Wehelie 2016; Brincat 2019; Shiakallis 2019; Jason and Wilbekin 2019; Rolinec 2019): an all-Black heavy metal scene that was covered in leather in an African desert.

The argument for exoticizing is further evidenced by the fact that much of the coverage has to do with visual aesthetics – a peculiar fascination with leather – as the musicians are rarely mentioned in the writings, less so shown in the photographs. For the photographers, the othering of the Botswana heavy metal scene has occurred because these are metal fans that have crossed into a subculture that has primarily been understood and accepted as traditionally White and Western. The roots of these assumptions stem from rock music's association with Whiteness, a result of what Paul Taylor calls the 'Elvis effect' (Taylor cited in Schaap and Berkers 2020: 3). Julian Schaap notes, 'rock music's whiteness can mainly be attributed to the interplay of social conditions in which it sprouted and, subsequently, the growing media industries which fostered its rampant growth between 1955 and 1957' (Schaap 2019: 89).

The origins of heavy metal in Europe has also shaped the discourse that the genre navigates, namely that of a culture informed by White perspectives and their struggles through Western middle-class life. Like any other African nation, Botswana's metal scene provides the metal world with a new set of perspectives, which are now amplified through riffs of their own. 'White' music has been a trivial categorization as much as 'Black' music has because none of these terms defines what type of music would otherwise be associated with these constructions, except merely an interpretation of who is supposed to be performing musical styles that are based on a Western behaviour of racial thought (Kendi 2019: 95). Bonet's words, like Marshall's (see Marshall 2012), have stated this genre's entry into Black Africa came as a surprise to them.[15] By acknowledging these differences the photographers are acknowledging inequalities that this music claims not to notice (Rodriguez 2006: 648).

As one salient example, the photographers who have published these photographs of the Botswana metal fans had not previously published photosets of rockers in Western markets and settings (though Bonet had previously directed a music video for seminal act Motörhead). I must also note that the outlets publishing the various photograph sets generally do not publish heavy metal related stories. This gazing by non-metal fans on a genre that is seldom accepted into mainstream dialogues also lends itself to a form of assumed parody. Some of the othering that has occurred by Westerners may in fact be tied to the image that non-metal fans have of the genre, one that fulfills a stereotype of deviancy and follies of obtuseness.

This marginalization of Batswana subjects shown in the photographs is not allowing them to be viewed as equals to their Western counterparts. Much of this is a result of White privilege, which is also a curious extension of the color-blindness phenomenon since 'Whiteness is used as the standard for behavior, appearance, and interaction in our society' (Donnelly et al 2005: 10). Thus colour-blindness is only validating White norms as well as the manner in which people who are not White and not Western are seen. This is the inequality that has been placed on the Botswana heavy metal scene as it is being viewed under the lens of Western norms, without regard for any cultural inclinations and proclivities that would accompany a set of metal fans in Botswana.

One of these is not like the 'other'

The global interest in the Botswana scene and the primary focus on the fashion of its participants is peculiar. The Botswana metal scene's association with leather is not exclusive to them, even as it has become their identifying feature. Metal scenes around the world have long been associated with specific fashions, including leather jackets and notably T-shirts adorned with a favourite band's logo. Another example of note that metal fans around the world have long taken to wearing are what are known as battle jackets: denim vests adorned with patches and pins which have become synonymous with heavy metal fandom (see Cardwell 2017). Corpse paint, represented by a face painted entirely in white in order to replicate death, often highlighted with black patterns that individualize the performers aesthetic, also serves as a mark of metal's fandom as it portrays a powerful visual aesthetic among fans of black metal, an extreme subgenre – perhaps the most extreme – of heavy metal with Scandinavian origins (see Kahn-Harris 2013) that has now spread globally, including the Batswana act Raven In Flesh.

Regardless, the chosen attire of metal fans in any number of scenes and sub-scenes varies around the world (Epp 2017: 84). Clothing, whether it is a T-shirt, battle vest or full leather cowboy aesthetic, serves to link metal fans worldwide in a manner that reinforces the genre's greater global community. Botswana's heavy metal scene, however, is the very first African scene to be documented for a global audience, and it has been done so solely for its visual aesthetics. It could be argued that the presence of heavy metal in Botswana is incongruous to the expectations of Africa in Western minds, perhaps explaining the amount of attention brought to this particular country's metal scene. Heavy metal's existence in both Western and non-Western markets has long existed and has seldom received coverage by the mainstream press. So why Botswana?

Saliently, MaRock photosets have showcased their over-the-top, ostentatious, leather adaption of a metal fashion by MaRock who have made this visual aesthetic their identity. Shiakallis says that throughout his time with MaRock, he was able to discern that fans had in part wished to emulate their metal heroes – Motörhead and Judas Priest, the seminal British band whose frontman Rob Halford emulated was typically photographed in leather – as well as the cowboy fashion of local farmers, whom Shiakallis feels are replicating American cowboy culture (Shiakallis 2019).

> They are authentic in that they created their own sense of style that is even as from now evolving into something quite unique [...] Other than the full leather/cowboy combination, they are creating these king-like crowns and angel-like wings as extensions to their outfits.
>
> (Shiakallis 2019: n.pag.)

My fieldwork in Botswana has also informed my view that using leather as a visual mark of metal fandom was a trend that began with fans emulating the images of the bands that they were enjoying. But these images of MaRock were not viewed in the manner in which a metal fan from a Western country wearing a leather jacket would be. Fans attending a metal festival in Western scenes would never receive any press coverage for doing so either. As McGrath says, the photographs and overall coverage has misrepresented the Botswana metal scene because it favours 'an exoticized distortion' where the fans and artists within the scene are being 'treated as an alien other [...] unworthy of genuine engagement' (McGrath 2015: 217).

Outside looking in

One particular article highlighting Botswana's heavy metal scene that caught my attention, for the very reason that it draws attention to the scene's othering and other academic themes, comes from the British magazine *huck*, which ran a feature on the MaRock scene for its 2017 'Outsider Issue', accompanied by the photography of Bonet. Author Bongani Madondo, a writer based in South Africa, leads the reader into thinking that this is yet another story about how peculiar it is to see metal fans adorned in leather in an African desert: 'It is explicitly for *listening* but, like the best of metal, it's a sight to behold' (Madondo 2017: 29, original emphasis).

After professing his naïveté of MaRock metal culture, Madonodo continues stereotyping of the scene in his article by stating the metal fans, whom he refers to as 'throwbacks', are conflicting an existence: 'Even a cursory listen to bands like Rokara, Evergreen, Dust N Fire and Remuda reveals a serious culture clash: the unapologetic sound of appropriation and reclamation' (Madondo 2017: 29). It is the use of the term 'appropriation' here that is a curious one, as the hinting of an appropriation insists that the metal fans of Botswana were merely borrowing the metal genre, instead of having embraced the genre for the enjoyment of the music. Madondo's assertion implies that the fans' interest in the music is perhaps not genuine. Ziff and Rao argue that appropriating a culture is a form of 'taking' from one that is not one's own, including 'intellectual property, cultural expressions, artifacts, history and ways of knowledge' (1997: 1). But, as discussed throughout this book, cultures and ideas are non-exclusive and thus syncretic to other ideas and interpretations. Botswana fans are not appropriating the culture, they are embracing a global heavy metal culture as their own.

What is not being discussed is that these images capture an embrace of a culture that has been shaped after decades of sculpting by fans and musicians, whose origins are otherwise viewed as a counter-culture to its surroundings. Heavy metal's culture came to life in the working-class capitalist British midlands and reflected the working mentality of its unofficial forefathers, Black Sabbath. Much like the rockers captured in the photographs, the images, too, are capturing a middle class in moments of exhale – stepping away from the mundane and the routines that would otherwise form their identity. Richard Rogers says movements, such as the embrace of heavy metal, are natural because it best reflects the participant's space. He writes that: 'Acts of appropriation and their implications are not determined by the intent or awareness of those engaged in such acts, but are instead shaped by, and in turn shape, the social, economic, and political contexts in which they occur' (Rogers 2006: 476). Rogers identifies four types of cultural appropriations, which include 'cultural exchange, cultural dominance, cultural exploitation (and) transculturation' (2006: 477), the latter of which, Rogers says:

> Involves cultural elements created through appropriations from and by multiple cultures such that identification of a single originating culture is problematic. Transculturation involves ongoing, circular appropriations of elements between multiple cultures, including elements that are themselves transcultural.
>
> (2006: 491)

This idea of a cultural hybrid that is able to easily travel serves heavy metal well when one considers that the genre was born from a form of appropriation itself: as the sculptors of heavy metal, Black Sabbath, cite their roots within the framework of the Mississippi Delta Blues and the influential guitar music that was born from the struggles of the first generation of freed Black Americans. James Lull states that transculturation is 'a process whereby cultural forms literally move through time and space where they interact with other cultural forms and settings, influence each other, produce new forms and change the cultural settings', thus possessing the ability to produce cultural hybrids (2000: 242–43), such as African heavy metal. Hybridity is best described as a form of culture that is adapted, blended and continuously renewed (Kraidy 2005: 16). As discussed in the first chapter, Arka'n Asrafokor's music is a strong cultural musical hybrid of their Togolese traditions and

Western heavy metal influences. The rise of metal in Botswana reflects a cultural hybridity that is a visual one.

This idea of varied cultures permeating through the established ethos of heavy metal has greatly impacted how the genre has become a borderless phenomenon, or as Paul D. Greene describes it, an 'ultraculture' (2011: 134). If not for this boundary crossing, heavy metal does not survive. Its own adaptations in the nations outside of the Western periscope is what allowed this genre to thrive. Postcolonial Africa is no different. The very reason why this genre has been adopted by fans in Botswana is because of the need to not only call the genre their very own in a country that has been increasing its global profile since raising its own flag but also because of the fans' desire to connect to a larger, global subculture.

Madondo embodies a very pan-African view of the metal scene in Botswana, in which his expectations as a Black African of the scene are not met because the metal culture in this African nation still very much resembles the metal culture of Western nations. This has led him to patronize the participants in a manner where he condemns the sounds to be those of a cultural appropriation, which in the case of heavy metal, is a Western replication. One thing he is not understanding is just how metal was able to capture an audience in Botswana, much less any African nation, exactly by replicating or appropriating the manners of their heroes.

One issue that Madondo's article highlights (and which no other article on the matter had previously done while covering this subject) is to acknowledge the idea of othering in his article by stating rather facetiously that the musicians and fans of the 'freakish novelty' that is the heavy metal subculture in Botswana, are on display:

> But globally speaking, it's [the Botswana metal scene] revered for the wrong reasons. Northern hemisphere media outlets in particular tend to regard the subculture as a freakish novelty: *Metalheads in Africa! Who knew?* [...] While Botswana's metalheads are charmed if not surprised by the attention, they're not at all bothered by the fleeting gaze of fame. They are all aware that they're being used as fodder and filler: fawned out for their *otherness*.
>
> (Madondo 2017: 29, original emphasis)

But for those unaccustomed to this subculture, the focus on the 'exotic' or 'others' has been the driving focus, especially when considering the chosen attire of the rockers, which is likely the primary reason so much attention has been placed on the scene's fans and less so the musicians. Of this idea, Marshall says too many media outlets viewed this story as a novelty, thus providing an attractive narrative for audiences who would otherwise not read about heavy metal. 'Overall it was viewed as a phenomena or kind of antithetical for a metal scene like this to exist in such a conservative and discrete African country', says Marshall (2019: n.pag.).

Shiakallis also states that there was a view that struck him as peculiar, as once his photo set – *Leathered Skins, Unchained Hearts* (2015b) – was published, he felt that this had already been 'old news', because of the attention that Marshall had already received for his *Visions of Renegades* set. Fearing a bit more at play than just another light bringing the Botswana metal scene into focus, Shiakallis feels that this story worked out well for media agencies as an entertainment story, less so than an informative story that would serve to provoke a discussion among audiences. 'I feel when you over glamourize something you create a passing trend', he says (Shiakallis 2019: n.pag.). Furthermore, Shiakallis feels that the reason the scene has received the coverage that it has is because of the skin colour of the subjects: 'That Black Africans are involved in the heavy metal scene, this is generally uncommon, as the general perception is that metal heads tend to be white' (Shiakallis 2019: n.pag.). It is impossible to ignore that the skin colour of the subjects likely plays a part in how Western audiences are hearing African heavy metal, nonetheless viewing this scene. Viewers cannot help but notice the skin colour of the subjects of the photographs as 'people direct their attention to it as a significant symbol' (Kotarba and Vannini 2009: 104) upon their first glance.

This dynamic of race contributes to the construction of the coverage in multiple ways, even from the lens of a Black photographer. Consider the photographer Lee-Roy Jason and his photo set of Batswana metal fans published on the Afropunk website in July of 2019 (see Figure 3.3). A Black South African (the only photographer of colour to document the MaRock scene), Jason travelled to the annual Overthrust Winter Mania Metal Festival in Ghanzi (a popular site for the recent wave of photographers; see Figure 3.4), where he describes the drive into town on the day of the festival with a heavy ethnocentric bias:

> Looking through the window while driving through this small town, happily taking it all in I spotted a Black couple buying veggies from a local vendor draped in leather and chains, confident and comfortable as if they had just stepped off the *Thunderdome*[16] [Miller and Ogilvie, 1985] movie set. That's when it hit me fully that I was in another realm. Eccentric is the standard here so I knew right there and then that I was in for a visual treat.
>
> (Jason and Wilbekin 2019: n.pag.)

Lee-Roy Jason's portrayal of the festival attendees informs the reader that he was departing his norm, entering a world where subjects – metal fans – were

FIGURE 3.3: Two MaRockos at the Overthrust Winter Metal Mania Festival in 2019. Photo by Lee-Roy Jason.

FIGURE 3.4: *Hangman Overthrust Metal Fest*, 2019. Photo by Andre Badenhorst.

the attraction, an amusement where he could gawk. This evokes the imagery of one of the more disgusting and horrendous stories of history: human zoos. These spectacles were designed to ostracize, demonize, fetishize, exoticize and marginalize citizenry in non-Western corners of the world, an effect which assisted in bolstering the case of colonialism for many leaders in the colonizing world.

Though I must state that I am in no way accusing Jason of swimming in the mindset of a colonizer or even toying with any ideas of superiority, his is nonetheless a careless choice of words. Jason's view of metal is ethnocentric, as evidenced by his thoughts that the genre of heavy metal, one that he feels is 'synonymous with white skinheads' (Jason and Wilbekin 2019: n.pag.), and was now being enjoyed by a group of devoted fans in a primarily Black African nation. While he states that the genre's reach into Africa breaks a stereotype, Jason falls into the trap of presenting the subjects as exotic figures at which he was able to gawk, evoking the rhetoric and philosophy surrounding the ugliness of human zoos. Of this phenomenon, Alexander Trupp says:

> From the eighteenth to the early-twentieth century, a form of public exhibition in which the objects of display were 'real people' gained worldwide popularity. These colonial expositions, taking place all around the world, from New York to London, Vienna, Moscow, or Tokyo, were exhibiting 'otherness' by emphasizing physical and later politico-economic and socio-cultural differences of the displayed persons who were often 'imported' from overseas colonies.
>
> (2011: 139)

It is difficult for the photographers to place the images in a way that puts their work into a different light, mainly because the audience is seeing what it wants – regardless of their intention. Shiakallis says that his work was never meant to 'glamourize', but rather to inform and educate the public of a different aspect of the scene by placing women at the centre of his work. Yet he understood that Western audiences were drawn towards a more intriguing visual, 'that the big draw card outside of the leather was that black Africans are involved in the heavy-metal scene' (Shiakallis 2019: n.pag.). Aldo Brincat, who concedes that his attraction to MaRock was a result of their 'theatrical manner'[17] (2019), says that he set out to eliminate a potential 'white gaze' by listing the Motswana names of his subjects as well as including a 150 word narrative by the subject who appeared in the photo next to it during his exhibitions (Brincat 2019: n.pag.).

Petra Rolinec also confronted a personal dialogue on the manner in which she feared her photography would be perceived, mainly because there has been too much focus on the metal scene's aesthetic. Rolinec instead hoped to convey a more human representation, a focus on the people behind the leather. Recalling her first encounter with local metal fans, she says they left her curious as their presentation did not match their demeanour. This led to her pursue a different angle:

> In my first meetings with them, I realized that what I really would like to show is the people behind the movement. I didn't want to focus on their appearance but on them as human beings. On their interactions with each other and the community that seemed to share a bond of love and kindness [...] People will always gravitate towards photographing the 'unusual' and considering that heavy metal is generally viewed as a rather 'white' genre it seems utterly ordinary that so many would choose to portrait [sic] the MaRock. I hope that my images fall a little bit out of that ordinary framework, but it is upon the audience to judge whether I managed.
>
> (Rolinec 2019: n.pag.)

One commonality of note that many images of MaRock have, is that they are often presented within the framework of physical strength, steering the viewer away from the independence that likely drew the fans to the genre. Batswana bodies are displayed in poses that frequently show them flexing, or in a power pose, often with mouths agape in a scream. Seldom are the fans presented in spaces that show them enjoying the music that shapes their identity as well as their sense of community.

Though some photographs, notably those of Rolinec and Bonet, appear to show MaRock within the spaces of live heavy metal performance, the other photographers – based on what was published – have not done so.

While fans are the immeasurable contributors in every heavy metal scene, the almost exclusive focus on the fans in Botswana illustrates an ulterior motive from the photographers as their work beyond the musicians highlights this cause. Placing fans of a genre of music in spaces outside of where this music is consumed is not only problematic, it can also be patronizing.

In the explanatory essay to *Foreign Nationals* (Brincat 2018), which was published on his website, Aldo Brincat writes that he took the photographs of rockers (about whom he said he once had apprehensions, as he perceived them to be 'evil' and 'racists' [Brincat 2019: n.pag.]) outside of an abandoned brick factory. Brincat says that he chose the specific site because of its ode to industrialism – describing it at a 'photographer's theme-park location', motivated by his intention of bringing 'theatricality to the fore' (Brincat 2019: n.pag.; see Figure 3.5).

Daniel Tamagni's (2013) photographs also framed MaRock outside of metal spaces (see Figure 3.6), much like Shiakallis, by encasing their subjects in the mundane, presenting some of their subjects in their own homes. Shiakallis's set, *Leather Skins, Unchained Hearts* (Shiakallis 2015a, 2015b; Kelly 2018: 70–72),

FIGURE 3.5: *Dictator* from Brincat's 2014 *Foreign Nationals* series. Photo by Aldo Brincat.

however, exclusively focuses on 'MaRock Queens', the women of the scene (see Figure 3.7).

Shiakallis' shots of the women indoors are meant to elucidate a more metaphorical approach, as placing the Queens 'in more closed-off domestic environments [...] emphasize[d] their societal caging. A few [...] so badly wanted to pull Devil's horns or pull an aggressive face, stand in a position so typical of the MaRock men. But that did not interest me', he says (2019: n.pag.). His intentions were to step away from the masculinity that the scene was already emanating, to show how women were using heavy metal to scale the walls of what he feels is a strong sense of patriarchy within the nation (Shiakallis 2015a).

Of the musicians featured in one of the photo sets, Vulture, vocalist of the Ghanzi-based death metal band Overthrust, has been photographed more than a handful of times, notably by Bonet (Wehelie 2016), though he is seldom captured in performance. In one instance, Vulture is seen standing on a motorcycle, pointing

FIGURE 3.6: An image from Daniele Tamagni's *Afrometals* 2013 series taken in Gaborone. Photo copyright Daniele Tamagni. Courtesy of Giordano Tamagni.

in the opposite direction of his gaze, which is focused on the viewer (see Figure 3.8). Instead of being viewed for his work in giving the music from the Botswana metal scene a larger profile, he is being showcased as a model in an art exhibit. For Vulture, however, he feels this representation was designed to show how varied scene members are, as it communicates 'different talent, character and lifestyle of individual metalheads, for example myself as a biker and others as cowboys' (Vulture 2020: n.pag.). He adds that fashion is vital to the Batswana metal subculture because it highlights an aspect that identifies this scene in a manner unlike any other in the whole world:

> Botswana is a natural-cattle rearing and farming nation. We ride horses taking care of cattle, design leather outfits from cow skins and decorating our yards with cattle products especially at the cattle posts [*sic*], such as cow horns and skulls.
>
> (Vulture 2020: n.pag.)

FIGURE 3.7: *Ludo Dignified* from Shiakallis's 2015 *Leathered Skins, Unchained Hearts* series. Photo by Paul Shiakallis.

FIGURE 3.8: Vulture, of the band Overthrust, poses for Pep Bonet's 2017 *The Hellbangers* photo series. Photo by Pep Bonet (Noor Images).

As a result of this visual, the Batswana heavy metal scene exist as nothing more than a mere novelty for spectators around the world. This phenomenon is not the result of the photographers (though they could have done a better job at representing the entirety of the heavy metal scene), nor the press, nor the subjects; this is a composite result of the ethnocentric and curious biases that Westerners have been informed by their whole lives when it comes to viewing people in non-Western settings. Westerners have long taken the accomplishments of Africans as a novelty: whether it is literature, poetry, cinema, innovations or medical advances, African contributions have seldom gained validation from the West because Africa has yet to be seen as a continent whose post-colonial existence has been viewed subjectively. Viewing Botswana, as well as Africa, in an unbiased, none-othering manner is what needs to change before the attention can shift towards the musical contributions of this metal scene.

They listen to Metallica in Africa?

Though Said argued that cultures were 'a matter of [...] appropriations, common experiences and interdependencies of all kinds among different cultures' (1993: 262–63), his ideas in *Orientalism* posits that Westerners are in need of reinforcing their own cultures, their norms and their ways, and thus point towards non-Westerners exercising similar interests in a manner which is beyond exoticizing: it patronizes their participation. For some, the images of the fans in Botswana were taken as a disruption to a stereotype held by many of not only what Africans could be like or look like, but of what Africans should look like and how Africans should behave. In part, this is also an ethnocentric construction of an African reality.

Ethnocentrism is the idea of viewing a culture and its practices from a biased perspective. Think of religious missionaries determined to spread their religion because they feel that another culture is worshipping and practising their religions and norms in a way that does not suit the missionary's views, thus the need to judge and eventually transform, or convert said culture into a manner that the missionary sees as more suitable to their ideals. Cultural relativism would best describe the opposite of ethnocentrism, as it observes a culture or a set of practices without bias; instead it relies on asking 'why' cultures do things and 'how' they are done. This dictates that observers at work can relay their observations for the purposes of research and information without providing their intended audience with an objective report. Cultural relativism informs much of academia and journalism, as both are professions where the story and idea take centre stage. Much of the work by these photographers, however, is valuable as it could be seen as the work taken on by an anthropologist for the sake of documenting a subculture. Hal Foster argues that artists, in this case the photographers, are capable of crossing into the world of anthropology because of their focus on a particular culture and their need for the work to be done in the field. From my interviews with the photographers, the work of Marshall, Brincat, Shiakallis and Rolenic was done by way of immersion within the country, with Marshall being the only photographer fully immersed in the scene as a metal fan. For others, their visits are ephemeral and relationships more professional – a fleeting immersion – which takes the viewers through a stock of fashion photography, and less so provides them with an insight into a subculture.

This fleeting immersion, Foster says, can be detrimental to othering the subjects and the implanting of the self from the perspective of the artists (1995: 307). By doing so, the artist runs the risk 'of a blind projection of the self into the other, or, indeed, an implosion into self-absorption' (Chikha and Arnaut 2013: 663). These photographers are themselves producing their own culture, likely through an ethnocentric bias, instead of documenting one that already exists, a phenomenon that would best be described 'in analogy to a theatrical producer' (Fabian cited in Chikha and Arnaut 2013: 666).

Like othering, ethnocentrism pulls the ideas of the viewer against their own understanding of what is to be expected versus someone else's lived experiences. Ethnocentrism is an assumption. Othering is ethnocentrism: it still reinforces an idea that 'they' are not like 'us' and 'their' actions should reflect what 'we' expect of 'them'. The photographs have provided the gazes necessary to reinforce our Western biases. Ethnocentrism has likely factored into why Botswana's scene has received the coverage that it has. Ethnocentrism is the inability to understand that your way of experiencing the world is not the only way. As Magnus Nilsson writes, 'this ethnocentrism runs the risk of producing too strong a focus on what sets heavy metal in Botswana – as well as in other African countries – apart from heavy metal in the Global North and, thus, in its misrepresentation' (2019: 187).

Until the initial publication of Marshall's work, the metal world had yet to see or experience an all-Black heavy metal subculture. This 'freakish novelty' (Madondo 2017: 29) was of interest to non-African press because it was unlike anything ever seen from Africa before, a show for the whole world, a step away from an ethnocentricity of assumed African narratives into Western ambitions. These images of the metal fans did not jibe with the West's conjuring of how the citizens of Botswana should be (Kotarba and Vannini 2009: 130). Whatever ethnocentric constructions exist about Africa, Botswana is a nation that has defied many assumptions about what an African country is supposed to be. This landlocked country of just over two million was cut off from the British in 1966 with over half of the population living below the poverty line, yet today sees its citizens enjoying some of the best infrastructure, health care and education in the continent, with its best students – including some in the metal scene – having received aid to study overseas (Ceasar 2020: 44; see also Acemoglu et al. 2001). Batswana are very much a part of the greater world around them, even if the world doesn't see their nation as part of 'us'. For the photographers working in the nation, Botswana was a soft landing, surrounded with Western familiarities and comforts.

Ethnocentrism exists because exoticism persists and because Westerners are continually othering the accomplishments, contributions and voices of Black Africa as a result of the loss of political control over former colonies, and as a further implementation of reminding those in the Global South that their accomplishments can never be measured equally against anything, that is, Western. This mindset has affected the struggles and ambitions of the post-colonial continent.

Those who have seen the photographs that have emerged from the Botswana metal scene may have garnered a false perspective of the scene itself, assuming that it is a healthy, vibrant scene whose performances are well attended and whose bands are achieving global success. Since my initial trip to Botswana, I do not feel that the scene has stepped forward in terms of gaining new fans. The Botswana metal scene has reached its local cap in terms of fandom. The distraction that the continual publicity of Botswana's scene has caused for the musicians attempting to push themselves to international audiences, has also allowed some musicians to remain stagnant.

Giuseppe Sbrana,[18] who fronts the band Skinflint, says that there has been an inaccurate portrayal of the scene caused by the exposure the leather-clad metal fans have received. 'The coverage is interesting from a visual standpoint, and may give one the impression of a big flourishing metal scene, but the reality is that the local metal scene is very small' (Sbrana 2020: n.pag.). His band has been one of the few acts from Botswana that have performed beyond the national borders and one of three to perform outside of Africa. Having also been profiled in Barnett's original story on the Botswana metal scene (Barnett 2012b), Sbrana was optimistic that the national scene would benefit from the exposure that Marshall received for his original photoset, yet the flocking that resulted has annoyed him, like other musicians, who are feeling that more negativity has come with the attention:

Some of it is an annoyance from an artistic point of view. I have seen great local bands and also been on the receiving end of performing at local concerts where the documentary crew will be filming solely in the opposite direction into the audience, trying to get them to pose or some shit with little to no footage of the band. It feels like a fashion show, and it's been done to death. I am over it.

(Sbrana 2020: n.pag.)

It is my personal belief, from interactions and conversations with musicians in Botswana, that the increased coverage brought a specious set of expectations: notably that the musical world would now come in, pull them from the Kalahari and dump them on American tours supporting Metallica, or European festivals with Iron Maiden. This led many to speculate that money was coming, their bands would be enjoyed worldwide and that metal fans around the world would start recognizing their music and talent. The complete opposite happened. And most of this has to do with the reluctance of many of those who are documenting the scene to push forth and provide the acts with the music and business acumen that is necessary to grow a scene. Vulture disagrees, however, stating the while he once believed the coverage was a hindrance to the success of the acts, he has since changed his mind:

> Between 2010 and 2015 I was real worried that international media focus was more into brutal Botswana metalheads' attire than the music itself, and this took down the visibility or any opportunity for the bands to be exposed to the world. However that is not the case anymore. From 2015 we saw many international media houses now diverting their attention to bands, and that brought a positive change to our metal scene as we also saw the old bands that had disbanded coming together and rising to continue where they left off.
>
> (Vulture 2020: n.pag.)

Vulture does concede that more attention should be focused on the bands though, noting their reality of a small scene does not generally fit the image that many outsiders have of the scene (2020). And, if more could be done for the bands, their scene could perhaps be elevated. 'With more and more coverage bands will be able to be seen and maybe get record label deals and tours or even sponsors', he adds (Vulture 2020: n.pag.). Metal Orizon vocalist Dumisani 'Dumi' Matiha also says that photographs have helped the Botswana scene, providing exposure to Western markets for a few of the metal bands that would have otherwise never happened, had it not had been for the over-the-top behaviour of leather-clad fans.

> It's something beyond our control, and these guys are not in bands so it is difficult to complain about them. As you might be aware, most bands don't even dress like that. (But) we also have to be careful we don't push them away.
>
> (Matiha 2020: n.pag.)

With little music acumen available within Botswana, bands who wished to push their music into new frontiers began utilizing the South African rock and metal scene as an outside source of knowledge, a result of the success some South African acts have had in promoting their music and brand internationally and the number of touring acts that have added South Africa to touring itineraries. Acts such as Overthrust, Skinflint and Wrust have kept a strong relationship with their Southern neighbours, performing as often as they could in a setting that offered new levels of professionalism, with public address systems that are suitable to international touring acts and further benefiting from a generous transfer of knowledge between South African acts and promoters. Understanding what was necessary behoved the Botswana acts who recognized that the attention from the global press was not for them, nor was it going to truly benefit them.

Skinflint, Wrust and Overthrust's entrance onto global stages has been remark-able to watch. Early press from CNN (Barnett 2012b), the BBC (Adepitan 2016), the *Wall Street Journal* (McGroarty 2016) and *The Guardian* (Banchs 2013) cata-pulted attention for these three acts. With the increasing media coverage, which includes several documentaries on the scene as well (Mosca 2014; Pyykkönen 2018; Vianney 2019), the bands never let this eye on the fans deter them from their work. They pressed on once they realized that their visions did not meet with the media exposure of the fans.

Overthrust (see Figure 3.9), notably, owe much of their achievements to the exposure as Vulture has embraced all that has come, including the visitors to

FIGURE 3.9: Ghanzi's Overthrust in 2019. Photo by Adrian Breda. Courtesy of Overthrust.

his Overthrust Winter Mania Festival. Furthermore, their presence in global markets, like Skinflint's, is showing other acts in Botswana what is possible. This newfound acumen has highlighted to aspiring musicians in the country what matters most and what it takes to get there (Matiha 2020). Concert promoter and manager Dave Israel says that Overthrust, Skinflint and Wrust have become 'role models' for local acts and aspiring musicians (Israel 2020: n.pag.). The presence of local talent ascending to larger global stages allows Batswana to no longer have to look at the Iron Maidens and Metallica's of the world to see what is possible.

Members of these acts are well aware of what they can bring back to Botswana. Sbrana says that touring Europe and the United States showed Skinflint (see Figure 3.10) how tough this business could be. 'It strengthens your resolve as a performer, both mentally and physically. No amount of rehearsals can give you that experience. It is vital to the growth of any band and will push you beyond your limits', (Sbrana 2020: n.pag.). Vulture also notes that what they have learned from the experiences of touring 'that side' have been brought back to Botswana.

> Their [Western] level of artistic professionalism is up to standard. Stage work, time management, sound and lighting is very important and should be given more attention. That we have brought it home and shared with our fellow metal bands and most of our shows have since improved a lot. Bands are giving their performances and there is [a] growth in upcoming bands.
>
> (Vulture 2020: n.pag.)

FIGURE 3.10: Gaborone's Skinflint in 2020. Photo courtesy of Skinflint.

Conclusion

The images of the leather-clad Batswana heavy metal scene depict a disruption of a stereotype, both from African and Western perspectives, of what heavy metal fandom could look like, versus what it is expected to 'look' like. As a result of the ethnocentrism, and the innate disbelief that a non-Westerner could also occupy a Western enjoyment much in the same manner that a Westerner can, an interest in this scene has led to a surge of attention for a story in Africa that does not fit the traditional rubrics of coverage for the continent by media outlets that would otherwise overlook a story about heavy metal.

Ethnocentrism, othering, fetishizing and exoticism were not the motivations of the photographers, however, the focus of their work may indeed appear to be so. Their interest in further documenting the scene was likely piqued after the publication of Frank Marshall's work. These photo sets of MaRock may have carelessly portrayed the subjects, as some have come across as caricatures of the local metal scene and in turn the global heavy metal subculture. Part of what may have driven this flocking was the interest from Western media outlets[19] that were quick to publish and document the scene themselves, driven by nothing more than Western gazes on something extraordinarily different: a result of othering.

At its best, othering serves as an entry point for a dialogue with a subculture or group that would otherwise be overlooked or stereotyped. At its worst, othering serves to fetishize or stigmatize a subculture or a group. With Western outlets and the photographers not recognizing metal's global reach, its impact, its acceptance and its passionate fanbases around the world, it is easy to accept the genre's arrival in Africa as a novelty. By doing so, Western intransigence provides an easy avenue towards othering, because the expectations of what is assumed to be African are not being met.

Heavy metal in Botswana is a product of expression, a reaction to globalization and the validity that many in the nation seek in the ever-expanding reach of a global musical genre, which is also in a constant state of evolution and has become a vastly diverse version of what it was when it first began. The genre of heavy metal has grown significantly since its inception by England's Black Sabbath, and it contains multitudes: everything from hardcore, folk metal, death metal, black metal, djent, groove metal and any other genre which may have come into existence since this sentence was typed. Heavy metal itself is also a hybridization, both musically and culturally, spawning and growing from the seeds planted by any musician with the imagination to think beyond the template stamped out by Black Sabbath.

In part the dialogue formed around the images resides in the expectations of what metal fans have traditionally looked like, as well as what the West has come to expect from Africans. The subject of the photographs has broken stereotypes and expectations by what they show – a metal scene that has blossomed and has been embraced by a population that heavy metal would have otherwise over-looked, but absolutely needs as a vital part of its evolution.

PART II

HEAVY METAL AND POLITICAL CONFRONTATIONS

4

Apartheid's Haze:
Finding Clarity through
Heavy Metal in South Africa

Though neighbouring Botswana's heavy metal scene has received a substantial amount of international press, the South African scene is the most successful in the continent. It is the African nation whose metal scene has produced the most international recording artists and touring acts, and it is the only nation in the continent that regularly receives well-established international touring artists. Further, this scene has come to life in the country that was one of the least likely to produce a metal scene in the sub-Saharan continent because of its well-documented political strife.

Today's South African metal scene exists in the shadow of one of the more embarrassing and horrific periods in African history: apartheid. Officially abolished in 1994, the systemic separation of populations based on skin colour had succumbed after international pressure and economic volatility forced the government to reconsider its villainous policy.

With its roots planted in the national dialogue since 1913 – following a series of Land Reform Acts – the policy of separation, or apartheid, became the official identity of the country after a 1948 election that saw the National Party (NP) emerge victorious on the heels of rancorous White supremacist rhetoric and fear.

For nearly 45 years South Africa existed as a nation with a fully implemented policy of strictly enforced institutionalized racism.

In order to validate the system of racial separation, an authoritarian government ruled with a heavy fist, draconian laws and despotic leadership. Every single South African who was White was born with an incredible privilege that not only benefited their citizenry but also established stronger financial advantages that were untouchable for the nation's majority Black population.

Non-White South Africans – which includes Cape Malay (descendants of enslaved Indonesians), descendants of Indian settlers, other Asian groups and Coloureds[20] (a term used to describe those of mixed race, and one that is still commonly used in the country today) – who in 1994 accounted for 87 per cent of the national population (Byrnes 1996), were treated as second-class citizens in the land of their birth.

Apartheid's ascension was a slow construction whose genesis came after the nation slipped away from British rule in 1910. Three years later, on 19 June 1913, with a single stroke of a pen, the Native's Land Act was passed setting aside 93 per cent of the land for the nation's White minority population. Seven per cent of the land was left to the nation's 67 per cent Black majority, who were also denied any rights of purchase from Whites (Bell 2013). Though there was a five per cent increase in the amount of land reserved for Black South Africans in 1936, this did little to help the plight of those searching for arable land as overpopulation led to soil degradation, disease and malnutrition, thus pushing many men into towns for viable employment, where they were needed to 'serve white needs' (Meredith 2007: 523).

More laws enforcing racial segregation would soon follow, including the Natives Urban Act passed in 1923, leading to the implementation of Pass Laws, one of the more poignant images of the apartheid era that would come in the following decades (Meredith 2007: 523). Pass Laws required non-White citizens to carry identification books (which resembled passports) when leaving their 'home-lands', even if for employment purposes, and to present these books upon request to police officers when stopped.

Apartheid's validation came by way of the draconian mechanism established and heavily enforced by the central government that used police and military as a full extension of the country's policies. Further validation for the system came from another source, one whose influence continues to linger South Africa: religion.

Religion's reach in the nation has shaped political and social dialogue since the arrival of the White settlers in the late 1400s and embedded itself culturally for the descendants of these early settlers, the Afrikaners, through the Dutch Reformed Church.

With the Dutch Reformed culture prominent throughout South Africa, the formation of the nation's heavy metal scene found its impetus during a troubling period when authoritarianism controlled the national dialogue. Furthermore, as the struggle against apartheid reached its apex and a transitional period loomed over the horizon, Dutch Reformed loyalists hammered down their waning authority by using heavy metal as a scapegoat. Concomitant with apartheid, the Dutch Reformed Church attempted to stifle the genre while inadvertently fostering heavy metal's spread, and its vestiges continue to be felt in the heavy metal scene.

This chapter discusses how a scene was able to carve itself out of a restrictive and omnipresent arm of politics and religion that reached into every aspect of national life. I have chosen to break the chapter down into three waves: rock's ascendency during the segregated state, the formation of the scene in the epoch that straddled the waning of apartheid and the years just after its end, and metal in the present – in a country that has found itself to be living with apartheid's religious and cultural vestiges.

First wave: Rebel minds, handcuffed hearts

Ethnomusicologist Charles Hamm explains that rock 'n' roll in South Africa, like it did elsewhere, provided the soundtrack of rebellion for youth looking to confront the preceding generation (1988: 19). As a generation in the United States was awakening to this new presence in its national psyche, it would not be long before the Western world caught on to this rabble-rousing raucousness stirring up American dance floors and generational ire everywhere it went.

Rock 'n' roll reached South African airwaves in the 1950s alongside its Western counterparts, signalling the 'contemporary issues and attitudes' (Hamm 1985: 159) of the time and the places in which this music was consumed. This style of music, born from African-American rhythm and blues only to be appropriated by Whites in the southern United States as their own, presented a welcome change and was led by something that few had heard on their radios to this point: the electric guitar. Early icons of the genre include Chuck Berry and Little Richard (both of whom were Black), as well as Jerry Lee Lewis, Bill Haley and Elvis Presley.

When this music reached South Africa in the 1950s it was the latter three that factored into influencing what was to come: only the White artists were being played on the radio, 'a decision made by record companies on the grounds that South African Whites were unlikely to respond to music by Black performers, particularly in the climate of heightened racial tension marking the 1950s' (Hamm 1988: 21). The censors of the South African Broadcasting Corporation (SABC), the national radio station that was controlled by the NP, were quite aware of the role this music played on the civil rights movement in the United States, and knew that it served as a symbol of unity for both Black and White musicians, who were well received throughout the country by all audiences.

However, the government attempted to deter South Africans from promoting Black foreign artists. As Hamm notes, the SABC refused to play rock 'n' roll at first before eventually allowing its airing because of competing radio stations from neighbouring nations whose signals could still be picked up in South Africa, notably LM Radio from Maputo, Mozambique, and ZQP from Lusaka, Zambia (1985: 160).

The government allowed the sale of rock 'n' roll in shops and its performance on radio, but the music would continue to be monitored for subversive content.

The government possessed the ability to monitor the entertainment consumed by the population through censorship of material it deemed inappropriate by way of the Publications Act of 1974 (Drewett 2003: 154), which allowed censors to monitor – not control – what was being read and broadcast on the radio (television did not begin broadcasting in South Africa until 1976[21]). The Publications Act succinctly outlined its adherence to religious principles: 'In the application of this Act, the constant endeavor of the population of the Republic of South Africa to uphold a Christian view of life shall be recognized' (Omond 1985: 201). Furthermore, the Publications Act's criteria for banning media that was 'undesirable' was done so because 'it or any part of it' was 'offensive or harmful to public morals, deemed blasphemous, or is offensive to the religious convictions or feelings of any section of the inhabitants of the Republic' (Omond 1985: 201).

Directions for screening music were outlined in a document containing thirteen guidelines for censors at the SABC to use when seeking out artists whose music should be deemed unsuitable. These guidelines were:

Swearwords are unacceptable.
The lyrics contain blatant unacceptable sexual references, which will cause offense.
The lyrics are in bad taste and cause offense.
The occult element in the lyrics are unacceptable.
The lyrics may inflame public opinion.
Unfair promotion of a political party or movement is unacceptable.
Lyrics propagate the use of drugs.
Glorification of the devil is unacceptable.
Blasphemy is unacceptable.
It is forbidden to use the national anthem in this way.
The SABS[22] believes the song is open to misunderstanding. The song has no positive message or statement against AIDS.
The impression of a Christ-figure, different to Christ, is found in the lyrics and is therefore unacceptable.
The total nihilistic approach is unacceptable.

(Reitov 2004: 85)

The Directorate of Publications would often respond to concerns from police officers, customs officers and the general public, who would then relay these concerns to the Publications Appeals Board, which was 'a government appointed committee designed to set aside or confirm the directorates' decisions' (Drewett 2003: 154).

Detailing her experiences as a state censor, Cecile Parker explained that lyrics for songs were examined for content that could be deemed detrimental to the state before passing them on to another censor:

> In between 1980 and 1990 there were generally about fifteen lyrics per week. If you take into account that we only, in those days, had about 480 LPs or CDs that came in per year, then it was quite a substantial amount of lyrics that had to be checked and voted upon. The voting system was open and my impression was that in those days virtually anything that was perceived as damaging to the state, to the SABC or to the NP, was regarded as not acceptable and we would ban it.
>
> (Parker cited in Reitov 2004: 83)

While the government held the power to censor artists whose music was a challenge to the political and social status quo, the bans only affected what could be played over the airwaves. Albums could still be purchased in record stores (Shoup 1997: 92). Some foreign record companies heeded the scorn of the NP and the Dutch Reformed Church because of the artists they were marketing, but they continued to sell records, reaping a substantial profit during the nation's postwar economic boom. Even as late as 1980, when Western companies were said to be complying with the boycotts of goods and services into South Africa, American record companies exported nearly four million dollars of recorded music into the country (Connelly 1982). Every musical trend that was happening in the United States and the United Kingdom made its way to South Africa as well (Schoonraad 2020); whether or not the political views of the record industry agreed with the politics of apartheid, the business model of apartheid – capitalism – suited Western interests accordingly. Black audiences were also included in the marketing of rock 'n' roll by way of 78 bpm records that were designed to be played on the battery-operated turntables commonly found in townships and informal settlements where electricity was not consistently available.

Further, bootleg taping was also widespread in South Africa, providing an outlet for marginalized citizens to purchase copied versions of the popular music of the era. Rock 'n' roll was often reviewed in the 1950s by Black newspapers such as *Zonk, Drum* and *Hi-Note!* which included write-ups on artists such as Bill Haley, Elvis Presley and Pat Boone among others (Hamm 1985: 167), even as the music thrived among Whites in the nation, and did so in a manner that accordingly promulgated its own rock-inspired music scene. Marketing attempts to reach non-White audiences stopped short when jazz found its way into the townships, in part because Black rock 'n' roll musicians were not marketed or sold in South Africa, and there is no evidence to support that albums by 'Chuck Berry, Little Richard, Fats Domino, the Platters, or any other black performers of the early rock "n" roll era were available in South Africa in the 1950s[23]; nor are these people mentioned in the press, white or black', (Hamm 1985: 169; see also Lulat 2008: 426). Rock 'n' roll, 'one of the first racially "mixed" music genres' (Bertrand cited in Schaap and Berkers 2020: 3), underwent a 'white-washing' – or, an 'Elvis effect' (Taylor cited in Schaap and Berkers 2020: 3). Since rock 'n' roll's realization as a commercially viable genre, its association as a 'White' genre has long been established – a notion not lost on American music executives, as one claimed, 'black rock won't sell to whites because it is black, and it won't sell to blacks because it is rock' (Mahon 2004: 68).

Non-White South Africans viewed rock music as an exclusively White and Western phenomenon (perhaps by design), which could have helped rock music serve as a unifying rally against the apartheid government. Instead it reinforced a cleavage.

Black South Africans found solidarity with jazz music, which developed a strong foothold among non-White South Africans for several reasons. Notably, there were strong political, economic and social similarities between Black populations in the United States and South Africa as both populations were engaged in a struggle for human rights (Coplan 1982: 122–23). Thus, Black South African music fans saw jazz as a reflection of their lived experiences and, in a sense, their voices. Because of this, South Africa gave birth to vibrant jazz scenes of their own with numerous musicians of note, many of whom were forced to live in exile as a result of their politics, including Hugh Masekela, Mariam Makeba and Abdullah Irbahim.

As apartheid's grip tightened over time, so did the manner in which Black musicians in the nation protested. Before the 1950s, protests came by way of traditional infusions into the music, as the state media was 'relatively tolerant of dissent in the 1950s' (Schumann 2008: 19) from Black musicians. However, this tolerance shifted during the later portion of the decade and onward as musicians were growing frustrated with the politics of the pass laws and the events of the Sharpeville[24] Massacre on 21 March 1960, where 69 people were killed by police forces during a protest of the pass laws that restricted Black South Africans from entering certain areas.

Black musicians now found themselves under greater scrutiny by the censorship board for fear of subversive lyrical content. Songs that were previously aired on the SABC and were once tolerated by the censors even though their lyrics were seen as subversive were now removed. To get around the censors, Black musicians used allegorical, humorous or sardonic language to navigate the waters of the censorship boards when it came to reflecting their lived experiences (Shoup 1997: 80). As singer Sipho 'Hotstix' Mabuse says:

> We would write songs in such a way that the officials could not detect what we meant in our songs. Because anything that would be seen as subversive would somehow

be banned by the SABC, and it was the only form of communicating our music to the public.

(Mabuse cited in Reitov 2004: 83)

White artists who challenged their government and its policy of segregation also found themselves up against the censors, including Roger Lucey, whose song 'Lungile Tabalaza' (1979) tells the story of an activist who died while in police custody. Lucey's albums were banned, his concerts were teargassed by police, and he faced numerous arrests, including one in his own home in the middle of the night. Owning a copy of Lucey's album could land the owner in jail for five years (Erasmus 2004: 76; Schumann 2008: 30).

For some artists, it was the sound of the music they were performing, less so the lyrical content, that was deemed troubling. During the 1980s, the NP's grip was watertight, ensuring that any inkling of Black culture remained separate from White minds. One notable artist of the time, and one whose popularity reached well outside of the country, was Johnny Clegg, who performed as a solo artist and in various incarnations of groups including Juluka and later Savuka. Known as 'The White Zulu', Clegg found allegory useful when approaching lyrics that undermined the government, ensuring that his music could reach audiences within his country, too. Furthermore, given his proclivity to use traditional Zulu music and the Zulu language, Clegg was viewed as a criminal by the state for appropriating Black South African music.

Recalling his time performing in Cape Town-based band The News, Robert 'Stretch' Schoonraad says his band learned firsthand how powerful the censors could be (see Figure 4.1). A new wave-influenced rock band, which touched on African rhythms, The News reached the national charts on the success of two singles, 'Up To No Good' (1981) and 'Station Road Rhythm' (1981), the latter of which was censored by the SABC, according to Schoonraad, for sounding 'too Black' (2020).

Songs were banned from most successful artists, both international and national, because of their higher profiles. Notable artists that received bans included Stevie Wonder and John Lennon, the former for acknowledging the struggles of Nelson Mandela during an internationally televised Grammy award ceremony, the latter's seminal classic 'Imagine' (1971) for asking listeners to imagine a world without religion. American singer Tracy Chapman's album Crossroads (1989) was released in South Africa without two songs, 'Freedom Now' (which was dedicated to Nelson Mandela) and 'Material World', that were deemed inappropriate and offensive to 'certain sections of the community' (Reitov 2004: 84).

Seminole British act Pink Floyd also confronted censors after Black students, rebelliously repeated a line from the band's hit song 'Another Brick in the Wall' (1979). The song's popular refrain, 'we don't need no education', was sung during

FIGURE 4.1: Cape Town's The News performing in the early 1980s. Photo courtesy of Robert Schoonraad.

protests by Black school kids to advocate better and equal education (Waters 2011: n.pag.). Infuriated, the government censors proceeded to ban the song, which was enjoying popularity during that time.

South African rock bands that were active during the 1970s included Raven, Suck, Stingray and the most successful act from the era, Rabbitt. These acts performed a mix of originals and covers and found success via radio broadcasts as a result of their apolitical music, notably Rabbitt, who scored multiple gold records in the country, including with their hit record 'Charlie' (1976).

It is apparent that the authoritarian state did everything it possibly could to ensure that no one in the country could access music that in any way would lead a population toward dissent – at least through public broadcasting. During apartheid, music was Whitewashed, cleansed of political appetites and dusted with the status quo. Those who spoke up loudly found themselves under scrutiny from their authoritarian government or forced into exile. It was during this political climate that heavy metal in South Africa was born.

In 1981, the act that musicians and fans in South Africa recognized as the very first heavy metal band stepped forward, the Johannesburg-based Black Rose (see Figure 4.2). Other acts that were also a part of this 'first wave' of heavy metal included Lynx, Pentagon, Razor, Vigilante, Nitro, Tyrant and Warlord.[25] But, with the arrival of Black Rose, it was apparent that they were the trend setters. Their music was a nod to their early rock 'n' roll influences, but with a new attitude, one being shaped by the wave of early British heavy metal influences and a working class – T-shirt and jeans – image that reflected who they were.

FIGURE 4.2: Johannesburg's Black Rose in 1982. Photo courtesy of Gary Walker.

These early metal bands would perform around the country in a rather extensive touring scene, with acts frequently taking residency in clubs for months at a time in various cities across South Africa. This scene was also fairly incestuous, as a few of the aforementioned bands featured the same members, sometimes due to members complying with the nation's compulsory military service[26] (with some returning to music, others leaving music entirely).

Musicians I have met and interviewed in South Africa (some of whom now reside outside the country) recall the early days of their country's metal scene as being difficult for two reasons: not only was the nation ruled by authoritarianism but the country was also dictated by a conservative culture that affected much of their everyday lives. Considering the strong authoritarian reaches and hovering censorship board, South Africa during the apartheid years was an unlikely place for a heavy metal scene to take root. Because of the constant surveillance from government eyes and ears, heavy metal in the country grew from the genre's cherished form of promotion: word of mouth.

Clive Pearson, formerly of the band Lynx, says that heavy metal came to South Africa late and likely benefited from Western expats settling in the country who brought new music and ideas to the music scene (2020). Marq Vas, a former vocalist of the band Metalmorphosis, also says that newly arrived immigrants from England, Scotland and the Eastern Bloc nations, who came to fill labour shortages, brought along new music and benefited from the connections they maintained with their home countries and the records and magazines they were being sent. 'We'd get to meet those kids at schools as South Africans and obviously they would share those records with us [...] that's how we got to know what heavy metal was about', says Vas (2020: n.pag.). For both Pearson and Vas, this connection provided them their exposure to Western bands that were otherwise unheard in South Africa, which included groups like Van Halen, Led Zeppelin, Scorpions, Iron Maiden and Metallica.

> As kids we thought bands like Budgie were heavy, and we thought Boston was hair metal and stuff like that. So when the kids brought the early Iron Maiden albums, like *Killers* (1981) [...] 'like oh my my god, look at that cover!' That wasn't even allowed in South Africa. You had to hide that away because that was banned. And eventually the record shops did start to release the stuff, mostly on import. So typically, the thrash related bands the Westerners brought across, especially the European bands. A lot of them started bringing the American thrash bands over the years, the Metallicas, the Anthraxs, the Exoduses and so on.
>
> (Vas 2020: n.pag.)

These albums mostly avoided the censors not only because they were mailed directly to individuals but also because they were not very commercially viable. In time, these records would become available for sale in the country, but there were challenges getting records into South Africa as much of what was able to be imported was still affected by international boycotts. Yet there were ways of securing shipments from the West. Jay R 'Sleaze', former owner of the defunct Johannesburg-based record store Total Chaos, explains loopholes were easily exploited:

> There was a lot of stuff banned by the government at the time like certain music, books and pornography. So there were no international labels with a South African division who would distribute a lot of metal, probably because it was banned or they didn't want to take the risk on it getting banned. The censors were pretty strict back then. I mean we would get movies released with scenes cut out because the censors didn't like them or deemed them morally corrupt. Anyway, turns out that at least for music and T-shirts, etc, [...] you could direct import without fear of it being seized. I had a contact for a distributor in London and we got everything through him. The first few shipments were a little touch and go, especially when they are held up at customs, but nothing was ever seized. I think it also helps that a lot of what we were bringing in was underground metal, so they probably didn't even know what they were looking at.
>
> (Jay R 'Sleaze' 2018: n.pag.)

Bands who chose to take their messages in political directions were often silenced by police forces. 'Where there were problems was with concerts that had a political agenda. There were a number of Free Mandela and End Conscription gigs that were shut down', recalls Gary Walker of Black Rose (2020: n.pag.). Metal was largely left alone during this era so long as bands kept their politics away from their lyrics. Often bands were monitored by plain-clothed police officers who would attend metal (and punk) shows to gauge what messages, if any, were being promoted by the performers. Recalling an instance in the mid 80s, Pearson remembers attending a concert in Johannesburg and having tear gas poured into the air ducts minutes after a band member shouted 'fuck the police' during their performance (2020).

Marq Vas also recalls that this was the norm in the scene during the late 70s and 80s, explaining that during his time as a performer in the 90s, the authoritarian presence had begun to dwindle. 'Police used to go and raid the gigs and beat up the crowds and put them in the back of the van and cut their hair. Did really crazy stuff: bomb it with tear gas, chuck the kids in jail without any rhyme or reason'(Vas 2020: n.pag.).

To circumvent the authorities, some metal shows, as with punk shows, were being performed on short notice, promoted by word of mouth. Others promoted out in the open, with only a semblance of information to keep police guessing. Yet, the police were never far behind. Dean Smith, of the influential thrash metal band, Odyssey, remembers receiving a notice and fine from the police for an upcoming show that his band was performing to promote an album release – the printing company had included their phone number on the poster (2020: n.pag.).

There was precedence for protest-led music during this period, notably with the *Voëlvry* scene of Cape Town that took hold in the late 1980s. Meaning 'free as a bird', this was Afrikaans language protest music performed with the intention of disrupting the status quo. For one of the scene's prominent players, Koos Kombuis, this was a 'fuck you movement' (Grundlingh 2004: 485). This scene, which also included Johannes Kerkorrel and Bernoldus Niemand,[27] performed rock 'n' roll 'with an overlay of punk, hard-hitting lyrics that satirized the state, Afrikaans political leaders, the South African Defense Force,[28] the apartheid system, and white middle-class values' (Grundlingh 2004: 485). This rebellion served to remind White South Africa that they, too, could very much be a voice of dissent for those in despair and that their existence could stand firm against the ills that their government created in the name of Afrikaans identity. It would be another decade and a half before another band with a punk spirit, Fokofpolisiekar, would come and sound the alarm for Afrikaans speakers. But the *Voëlvry* movement is remembered fondly because of the inkling of hope it provided and the template it set for how powerful electric guitar-driven music could be.

Heavy metal's nascence in South Africa was in a police state confined by an authoritarian and religious state – an unlikely setting to birth a metal scene. The end of apartheid was not only the start of an integration that was so desperately needed, but it also marked a liberation from the ever-ominous presence that lingered over the nation's shoulder. Artists seemingly had a burden lifted as their voices stood to be exposed without persecution, a platform that benefited artists and audience alike. For rock and metal fans, however, a peculiar era was just beginning.

Second wave: Die Duiwel se musiek

Apartheid's waning days triggered desperation in the conservative *Nederduitse Gereformeerde Kerk*, or the Dutch Reformed Church. The separation of church and state ushered in by the wave of democracy signified a transition away from authoritarianism, and a panoply of voices was hoping to continue their own form of control by way of moral entrepreneurs, notably a quixotic former police officer named Rodney Seal. By assuming the role of a 'moral entrepreneur' Seal stepped into the role of a 'do-gooder', an activist who created a personal crusade against a cause that he, himself, felt he needed to approach (Goode and Ben-Yehuda 1994: 154).

In linking rock and metal to Satanism, homosexuality and murder, Seal's crusade was intended to stigmatize the music enough to dissuade adolescents from listening to heavy metal by using what could be best described as a fear campaign, much the same way that the United States went through a moral panic, with heavy metal taking centre stage; in some U.S. cases, the genre's most recognizable stars were put on public trial, including Metallica (Karwath and Davidson 1987; Dolan 1987), Judas Priest (Victor 1993: 169–70; Philips 1990; Tepedelen 2018: 64), Ozzy Osbourne (McDougal 1986; Murphy 1986; Philips 1990) and Slayer (The Tribune Staff 2012; Martin 1997). Heavy metal has long found itself in the crosshairs of conservative fervour because moral panics have very much come to define an 'inherent component' of this genre's narrative (Klypchak 2011: 41).

Seal's warning came in the form of a book he published called *Rock Music and the Right to Know*[29] (1988), which became a valuable resource for parents and church members who pushed false pretenses about heavy metal. Seal also travelled around the country lecturing classes on the dangers of Satanism and presenting a list of known Satanists and homosexuals. His presentations were often complemented by music and videos from rock and metal artists spanning degrees of the rock spectrum, from Sting and Meat Loaf to Metallica and Cannibal Corpse. Seal's plan to sway potential listeners by playing heavy metal to students around the nation had an inverse effect of sorts, becoming a contributing factor to introducing new fans to the genre. Many teenagers around South Africa were exposed to extreme music for the very first time through Seal's presentations.

Seal's influence grew significantly, allowing for simulacrum courses to be replicated in schools around South Africa. Patrick Davidson, a blogger and musician based in Cape Town, tells of how the government's link with conservatism also introduced him to metal:

> The government had a strong tie with the white Afrikaner church, and it was compulsory in government schools that there were Bible classes in the curriculum. They would sometimes screen these Christian documentary-style films in Bible class about how evil bands were supposed to be. So it's no lie to say that school introduced me to metal at the age of 10 or 11 or thereabouts. Needless to say, those were my favourite classes. I don't think the church knew about death or more extreme metal in those days; they'd have a shit otherwise!
>
> (Banchs 2016a: 39–40)

'He did us a tremendous favour by what he was doing. He went to great lengths to find these bands', (Banchs 2016a: 37) says Christo Bester of Johannesburg grindcore act Groinchurn, who stated his knowledge of heavy metal only grew because of these appearances. Similarly, Anton de Willars, a Cape Town-based musician, explains that without question rock and metal were discussed with scorn by the authoritarian government and that much of their inculcations of how evil this genre could be was passed down through their education:

> I remember being given assignments at school where we had to research musicians – pretty tame stuff like The Beatles, Queen, Sting, Rolling Stones – and find and point out all the ways that they're trying to subvert our thoughts in order to brainwash us into becoming Satanists.
>
> (Banchs 2016a: 40)

What Rodney Seal did was construct an elite-engineered threat that created a moral enemy (Goode and Ben-Yehuda 1994: 164). Using his privilege as a former police officer, he was able to validate his fictitious claims, distracting a greater society from the other aspects of South African life at the time – a system of unwavering racism. Seal's career as a police officer only served as a validation for those who supported him. More importantly, his work and influence impacted law enforcement agencies with their efforts (Goode and Ben-Yehuda 1994: 164).

These efforts did not end with Seal's crusades. The South African Police Services also led a fear campaign by establishing the Occult Unit in 1992, the brainchild of Kobus Jonker. A born-again Christian and police officer whose nicknames included 'Donker Jonker', 'The Hound of God' and 'God's Detective', Jonker began taking an interest in the occult after supposedly witnessing a Satanic ritual. The unit, described as the 'world's only ritual murder' task force'[30] by anthropologist Annika Teppo (2009: 27), was linked with the powerful conservative Christian forces within the dominant White community in the waning years of apartheid.

Born from the doctrines of the Dutch Reformed Church, the Occult Unit, which was disbanded in 2006,[31] took precautions against the ills of Satanism by publishing a list of Warning Signs. Among the details included on the list: rejection of parental values, draping hair over the left side of the face, changes to the appearance of the child's bedroom and an affinity for heavy metal music (Kemp 2015). This placed metal fans and musicians in uncomfortable positions as they were now finding themselves in confrontations with a desperate group.

For some musicians like Marq Vas, who remembers a time when confrontations in the country were different, opposition to his music was one he embraced. Recalling a Metalmorphosis concert in the mid 90s (see Figure 4.3), Vas noted that protesters had gathered outside a venue in the city of Boksburg. Having been notified of potential protests beforehand, Vas arrived wearing a clerical collar and took to the stage while reading pages from pornographic magazines. Once he began to perform, he removed the collar and shirt to reveal an athletic jersey that he had personalized

FIGURE 4.3: Johannesburg thrashers Metalmorphosis in 1993. Photo courtesy of Marq Vas.

with the number '666' on the back, which did not sit well with those assembled. 'Right outside they were trying to kick the door in, which was wonderful media for us because next day it was in all the newspapers – pictures of me in the priest outfit' (Vas 2020: n.pag.). Vas's recollection of the fervour that ensued highlighted the spill-over after the transition from an authoritative government to a democracy, which was one of desperation from the nation's religious leaders. 'They'd lost grip [...] they needed something else to latch onto. We had an interesting time with the church', he says (Vas 2020: n.pag.). In his view, the Dutch Reformed Church was upset at the NP for 'selling out' in a sense, conceding that the economic and political segregation policies of the government needed to end (Vas 2020).

Nicky Falkof posits that much of this panic was born from the entertainment of an unknown culture swarming into a South Africa that no longer had any sanctions or restrictions. Likewise, the spread of underground metal likely assisted Seal's crusade to assuage concerned parents and citizens:

> Much of the fear surrounding Satanism was encoded in worries about foreign films and music, newly permitted in a nation that had, until fairly recently, maintained strict censorship and a prohibitive attitude to American and European cultural products: television for example, was only broadcast after 1976. By the late 1980s copied cassettes of foreign heavy metal bands spread like wildfire, fostering a growing gothic and heavy metal subculture. Black clothing, long, dank hair, pentagram symbols and other defiant adolescent affections became common and [...] served as a visual reminder that Satanists were 'out there'.
>
> (Falkof 2012: 6)

In 2008, a heinous murder would reignite the fears of religious conservatives, when, in the picturesque Johannesburg suburb of Krugersdorp, a samurai sword was used in the gruesome killing of a student[32] at Nic Diedrichs Technical High School.

What shifted this case into the international spotlight was that the culprit, Morné Harmse, wore a mask during his rampage that was meant to resemble one worn by Corey Taylor, the lead vocalist of the Des Moines, Iowa-based Slipknot, one of the more established international success stories in heavy metal. Slipknot is set apart from their contemporaries by the band's penchant for wearing individualized masks during their live performances. Harmse was also in possession of a bag that contained a few other swords, knee and elbow guards and three other masks, which were said to resemble that of another member of Slipknot. Local police also reported Harmse's affinity for Ouija boards and 'Satanic' music after searching his bedroom. The crime was described as a 'Satanic ritual' in a local newspaper (Grobler 2008: n.pag.) because another paper reported (through an unattributed quote) that Harmse believed 'Satan would kill him' if he did not commit the murders by the day's end (Plessis and Roestoff 2008: n.pag.).

Pierre Eksteen, a local social worker, was quoted as saying: 'He came here camouflaged as the guy from Slipknot. We know the wrong kind of music and drugs have bad effects. Young people need to be informed of the effects of bad Satanic music' (Michaels 2008: n.pag.), a sentiment that echoed the teachings of Rodney Seal a decade prior. The head of Krugersdorp's investigative psychology unit Gerard Labuschagne, however, quickly dismissed any correlations. 'Whenever there is a murder, people jump to conclusions, and always god or Satan told the killers to do it. These notions shouldn't be taken seriously because it is straightforward: someone, of their own free will, can kill another person' (Michaels 2008: n.pag.).

While Harmse detailed his affinity for the band and had listened to their music frequently in the months leading up to the event, he confessed that he killed his classmate and injured others for attention (Ndaba and Foss 2009), not because of any instructions he was receiving in Slipknot's music. The event, however, caused a national panic.

A few months after the Harmse incident, the American thrash metal band DevilDriver was forced to pull out of a festival appearance in the country over protest from religious groups, who pointed to the band's name (Channel 24 2017; IOL 2008) as a Satanic identifier (the California-based band is not a band that promotes Satanic ideology). More recent incidents highlight the stigma that heavy metal continues to carry beyond the apartheid era.

In 2015, the Witchfest Metal Festival, a multi-day heavy metal festival featuring international acts, was forced to change venues three times as a result of the protests held by religious groups (Pasbani 2015). In 2016 Greek death metal band Rotting Christ toured South Africa under a different name because of the scorn the band was drawing from religious protests,[33] which drew international attention. The concert's promoter, Shaughn Pieterse, told a British radio show these protests invoked the peak of religious hysteria from the government in the late 80s and early 90s (Lach 2016). Protests by the South African Council of Churches in Pretoria as well as conservative groups in Cape Town even followed pop star Lady Gaga during her 2012 tour of the country (Channel 24 2012).

Unlike their counterparts that activated the 'first wave' of metal, which was saliently marked by their lives under authoritarian rule, bands such as Vas' Metalmorphosis, Pothole, Ragnärok, Voice of Destruction (VOD) and Groinchurn among others in the 'second wave' acts were actively performing in the wake of the 1994 election (though some of them formed before this period). These acts were met by an overwhelming response from conservative religious groups that had lost their influence and thus sought to validate their existence by extolling their ways in opposition to a scene that they felt was vulnerable. It must be noted that these religious groups and moral entrepreneurs were acting on their own will and funds without government support, as the new, post-apartheid South Africa was now a secular republic.

Even without validation from the government, the Dutch Reformed Church was able to influence a case against heavy metal, painting it as a form of art that served as an introduction to deviancy and Satanism – a scare tactic that leveraged control back to the moral crusaders. Heavy metal's entrance into the dialogue of conservative leadership was in concomitance with nervous leaders during the time apartheid's grip was slowly loosening. The scare of Satanism was a response to a social change that came as 'a consequence of the fear of apartheid's end' (Falkof 2012: 7).

It was those in power who stood to lose. 'The possibility of blaming Satanism for personal and communal ills was only available to those who inhabited the spaces of privilege' (Falkof 2012: 19). With their power irrelevant, Church leaders needed to find other ways to validate their influence within the nation. A moral crusade was the best possible manner in which to reinvigorate their voice. Yet, like the institutional racism that plagued the nation for decades, this crusade proved to be a failure.

With their attachments to the Dutch Reformed Church, religious and political leaders and Afrikaner nationalists held their Bibles ever so tightly during apartheid's last days. Theirs was an identity of power, privilege and prestige. In the minds of Afrikaans leadership, they were *the* ethnic group of South Africa, and in a short time, they were to become just another cultural group in the nation.

The transitional years served to silence authoritarian voices while awakening new ones. With the nation's youth embracing their newfound freedoms, a void of expression needed to be occupied, one that could serve to reignite the confidence of a nation that was slow to hold its head up.

The untethering of Afrikaans and the screams of 'Fok of!'

Detached from the authoritarian milieu of their parents' generation, many Afrikaner youths, like any other ethnic groups, were eager to define their own identity in the post-apartheid country. However, for the Afrikaans, opprobrium shaped much of their identity, one that remained tethered to the church that defined previous generations and one that was looked down upon as a result of the national sins the nation was now tasked to heal from. This was a youth that was eager to break from the past and pull away to form an identity of their own.

It was during the late 90s and early 2000s that a new sound came about to help transform the youth's identity: Afrikaans-language rock music. The first rock band of note that garnered an audience was Springbok Nude Girls, an alternative rock band that formed in the early 90s in Cape Town, eventually signing a record deal with Epic Records in 1996.

However, it was another band with an unapologetic name and a cutthroat sound that would come to embody the identity and space that many Afrikaans youths were desperate to inhabit: Fokofpolisiekar ('Fuck off police car').

Formed in 2003 in the middle-class Cape Town suburb of Bellville, Fokofpolisiekar's tenacity in shaking up the old guard was unrivalled. Their brand of alternative rock struck the right chord with audiences across the country upon the release of their first album, the 2003 EP *As Jy Met Vuur Speel Sal Jy Brand* ('If you play with fire you will burn yourself'). My travels throughout Africa and Europe as a fan of rock and metal have never exposed me to a band whose sound and message meant so much to a particular culture and, to a further extent, a nation. Fokofpolisiekar's shows are an eruption of raw, tearful emotions (see Figure 4.4). Fans of music in the country, whether or not they were steady listeners of guitar-oriented music, have long expressed just how important this band was to the national dialogue.

Much of this was a direct result of the cultural attachment to the Dutch Reformed Church and the conservative history that has long been a part of

FIGURE 4.4: Fokofpolisiekar's Francois Van Coke in 2017. Photo by Wayde Flowerday.

Afrikaans identity. Fokofpolisiekar's arrival challenged those long-held beliefs of God and country within the Afrikaans history, bringing an entirely new dialogue to their culture.

The band's vocalist Francois van Coke says of their arrival on to the South African scene:

I don't think we ever realized that we challenged the church or the government, but we definitely rebelled against the norms of growing up Afrikaans. Religion is a big part of Afrikaans culture because of the strong held conviction they possess of a pact with God. We did not believe in that God and weren't scared of saying it.

(Banchs 2016a: 42)

The band was often confronted by the shibboleth of the old guard, especially after the national scandal that ensued when their bassist, Wynard Myburgh, autographed a fan's wallet with the message '*fok* god' ('fuck God') (Christie 2013: n.pag., orginal emphasis) – an act that led to numerous show cancellations and nationwide protests. Fokofpolisiekar was the band many feared years prior, one that could easily extend their hand to the nation's youth and lure them away from conformity and towards individualism. 'They went out of their way to break down those rigid cultural barriers to reject the stereotypical past and embrace the freedom to be yourself, in the company of whoever [*sic*] you choose', says Cape Town-based musician Adam van der Riet (Banchs 2016a: 42–43). For the post-apartheid generation, the 'Dutch Reform Church looked like an oppressing artifact from the apartheid era and they wanted nothing to do with an oppressing organization of any kind' (Klopper 2011: 185).

Fokofpolisiekar's liminal arrival allowed fans to smash their connection to the country's past. The band happened because their generation, 'Mandela's Children', was desperate to cultivate their 'ownness' – their own voice and their own identity.

There was also lingering guilt over Afrikaans identity in years after apartheid. Though it is difficult to gauge just how much the post-apartheid years weighed on the consciousness of the Afrikaans, my personal interactions with the cultural group highlighted that in the year afterwards, especially during the first post-apartheid decade, many shied away from this identity, going as far to change surnames to avoid being identified as Afrikaans and completely avoiding communicating publicly in the Afrikaans language, one that bore the burden of identity (Hoad 2014: 195).

The language was likely a rebellion against the colonial rule of the British, wherein a 'South African' government could rule the way they chose under their rubrics of culture and norms, including their African language. The NP chose to enforce the teaching of Afrikaans in public schools; favouring the English language was seen as an extension of colonialism. As such, Afrikaans was viewed as the language of the oppressors by Black South Africans (Shoup 1997: 75), and, for many cultural Afrikaners, the language becomes limited to home use and was seldom heard in public in the years following apartheid.

For native Afrikaans speakers, who came of age in the years after apartheid, understanding the shame of the nation and their culture's past, a confrontation was necessary to address issues of conservatism surrounding their culture, and music was the perfect vehicle. Annie Klopper details, 'they [Afrikaans youth] longed for the emancipation from the institutions and ideas that were forced on them by their ancestors, and "in ferocious anger bit the hands that control" by means of punk protest' (Klopper 2011: 185). The time was ripe for a voice to emerge from the stranglehold of apartheid, and Fokofpolisiekar[34] found it.

Third wave: Unchained hearts, open minds

Heavy metal's presence was quieter in the years after the 1994 election, which officially marked the end of apartheid and culminated with the ascendency of the revered revolutionary, Nelson Mandela, as the newly elected president of the nation. Full integration between citizens, though permitted, would take time as the scars of a bruised nation will take generations to fade. Black leadership brought both political and economic uncertainty to some Whites. At least 800,000 Whites have emigrated since 1995 (Economist 2008) to countries such as Australia, the United Kingdom, Canada and the United States.[35] Many of the nation's early rock and metal musicians also took flight.[36]

The South African bands that performed during this transition were slowly able to take larger steps and engage with a world free from economic and political boycotts. This was the first generation of South Africans in over 50 years to be able to embrace the world around them, and as such, have the world embrace them. Bands such as Groinchurn and Voice of Destruction jumped to sign international recording contracts with Germany's Morbid Records. Others including Sacraphyx and Agro also joined in performing in Europe, and both appeared at the legendary Wacken Festival in Germany.

With the scene now able to reach beyond its historically limited demographic, one major question remained for a citizenry rooted firmly in the modern state: Do participants in a genre that is rooted in Whiteness and maleness feel comfortable occupying these spaces and scenes?

While some remarkable strides have been made in the generation since the apartheid government stepped away, it has been almost impossible to quickly shake off the racial lines that were drawn during the apartheid era.

Mary Robertson, an ethnomusicologist who has studied the effects of race and music in the post-apartheid nation, says that in today's South Africa, music stands to reaffirm racial identities, continuing to carry racial labels – 'Black music', 'white music'[37] – much like it did during apartheid (2011: 460). Considering such labels, it is best to understand that metal and rock have long existed as a space of White voices around the world. Members of the genre's most successful bands, no matter their national origin, are predominantly White and predominantly male. Thus, the non-White and non-male stars in the genre, which are few, are 'hypervisible' (Hoad 2014: 190–91).

Without irony, the hypervisible in Western metal scenes are 'othered' because of their ability to cross the threshold into these traditional spaces. Though these musicians, notably Jimi Hendrix, Joan Jett, Phil Lynott (Thin Lizzy) and Alissa White-Gluz (Arch Enemy) are well-respected within this world for their work, seldom do fans discuss their contributions without discussing their non-White, non-male 'otherness', one that is necessary to maintain the scene's dominant, 'coherent scenic identity' of White-maleness (Thornton cited in Overell 2011: 213).

Why this Western dynamic matters so much in South Africa, a nation where over 90 per cent of the population is non-White (South African Government Census 2011), is because this is the only heavy metal scene in the African continent that is dominated by a minority White population. Beyond visibility, the racial composition here shows that the scene, unless it is able to expand beyond the presence of a White minority, will remain in stasis. This issue is not lost on South Africans passionate about metal. Though it would seem the best way to expand metal's reach to a non-White audience is to simply continue without a forceful push, allowing prospective fans to discover the music on their own, it will likely take some time before the demographic of those who claim metal fandom becomes a proportional representation of the national population. Metal in the nation today has become more accessible within South Africa as the genre has gained national access through more traditional platforms – television, print and radio – and a widespread internet reach.

Once at the centre of the apartheid resistance, Soweto Township today is now host to a variety of rock and metal acts including hard rockers Ree-Burth, skate-punkers TCIYF (see Monster Children 2019) and extreme metal standouts Demorogoth Satanum. The latter two of these acts have gained strong reputations within South Africa, and garnered strong fanbases both within and outside of the continent, with TCIYF having completed a European tour in 2019 (see Figures 4.5 and 4.6). The aforementioned bands are hypervisible within the scene as they are composed of all Black, township-raised members, whereas bands from the rest of South Africa are predominantly White. At the time of this writing, only a few notable bands in South Africa – including Deity's Muse, Facing The Gallows, 11th Hour and Vulvodynia – are among the bands that feature mixed-race lineups.

FIGURE 4.5: Soweto's Demorogoth Satanum performing live in 2019. Photo by Christelle Duvenage.

FIGURE 4.6: Soweto's TCIYF performing live in 2017. Photo by Christelle Duvenage.

Women, notably, are the scene members whose presence has increased in the years since the transition. The visibility of women in any scene comes with a set of expectations based on gender norms that have been passed on through patriarchal and societal constructions that exist in virtually every corner of the world. Thus, the perfervid patriarchy that lingers in a nation whose rule was once validated by the Dutch Reformed Church has been slow to ease in the post-apartheid state.

Masculinity's role in apartheid was central to upholding its political culture. Identity and race culture were also defined through this lens of masculinity during the apartheid era (see Epstein 1998; Mooney 1998). Further, as already discussed, the church and schools were also very much implicit in shaping Whiteness and maleness through discipline, and later in a male's upbringing through a conscripted military service. In a country divided by a policy of institutionalized racism, race was not only visible, it was a legal definition. Today, while the legal structures have erased such notions, the vestiges of such practices remain. Rock musicians during apartheid were not explicitly ostracizing prospective Black participants from the rock and early metal scene. However, it was the presence of White males, and what their privilege represented, that kept many prospective participants away.

It is society that defines masculinity, constructs its norms and its parameters of function as gender. Masculinity and gender, are, in a sense, a performance. South African masculinity has been defined by its former attachment to the Dutch Reformed Church, which reinforced a strong anti-homosexual agenda, and the political control exerted by men for men. Upon arrival to South Africa, rock 'n' roll succeeded because masculinity was able to be used as an aspirational template for behaviour through life in an authoritarian rule – a genre defined as a rebellion against a status quo which felt comfortable to its fans and performers because of its image, not because of its overt political messages. These performances of masculinity are social interactions that reinforced gender norms and hierarchy, triggering varying responses that served to inform various levels in the hierarchy of masculinity (West and Zimmerman cited in Vasan 2011: 337).

Heavy metal has also fallen into this trap of reinforcing masculinity given that the genre's norms and ideals have been established by men, often with more aggressively ferocious displays. As Walser states: 'Heavy metal is, inevitably, a discourse shaped by patriarchy. Circulating in the contexts of Western capitalist and patriarchal societies, for much of its history metal has been appreciated and supported primarily by a teenage male audience' (2004: 334). Furthermore, it must be stated that metal fans who identify as women have to 'embrace a seemingly one-dimensional and immoveable gender position', (Nordström and Herz 2013: 463), one that is ladened with hyper-maleness.

Natalie Cowling, a Johannesburg-based musician, says that the metal scene is very welcoming to women, however, she notes that any hesitations for women who would like to step into the local scene may arise from gendered constructions of the heavy metal culture, which does not view women as 'capable of possessing the characteristics associated with heavy metal – aggressiveness and independence – and behaving in a manner which is distinctively masculine. I think these elements are localized aspects within the sociology of the heavy metal subculture' (Cowling 2018). Cowling's perspective elevates a perception that masculinity in metal is a result of a construction surrounding gender, less so the attributes of the music (Hill 2015: 245), and that for women to successfully enter the scene they are almost forced to mimic the behaviour of men in order to gain the respect of the status quo (Vasan 2011: 335). Or, as Sonia Vasan elucidates, they gain acceptance by 'submitting to the masculinist codes of the subculture' (2011: 334).

Rock music since its inception has long been a male-centric performance, establishing how male patterns of thought and behaviour should be viewed. It is, as Robert Walser says, an 'arena for enactment of male power' (2004: 350). Rock music, it could be argued, has also helped shape the way that women are viewed: through its long history of misogynistic lyrical content, men have (nearly) exclusively constructed the dialogue of the genre through male aggression, competition and even through male fragility and sensitivity. Sara Cohen says that, though rock music may not be inherently male or reinforcement of gender roles, it is still produced through a male 'social practice and ideology', stating that through rock shows, both performers and audiences 'can adopt, create and recreate masculine roles and identities' (1997: 34).

South African music blogger Claire Martens states that the metal scene, like any music scene in the nation, is merely an extension of the way women are viewed in South African society as a whole:

Metal in [South Africa] is not a very masculine place specifically—not in a way that makes you feel excluded. There are some issues with men harassing women, but I think it's just a couple of people who don't understand boundaries. It follows the general greater societal experience of women. The problem with these men is that they are defended, and I really believe that we should be trying harder as a collective to root these people out. Metal should always be a place of inclusion, but sadly it is not.

(Martens 2019: n.pag.)

As Mavis Bayton says, guitarists are not born, they are created, stating that women's absences in rock and metal are entirely social (1997: 39). Thus, a woman's arrival into this male arena could not only signal a break in 'the gender code' (Bayton 1997: 43) but also be overshadowed by their gender. Women who do breakthrough, and are fortunate enough to earn a living performing, still have to undergo the challenges of sexism in the workplace that men are privileged to not have to endure:

> They encounter hostile male musicians, prejudiced promoters, patronizing disc jockeys, obstructive technicians who sneer and make sexist jokes at their expense, inhospitable masculist working conditions, unimaginative marketing by record companies, and sexploitative media coverage. They also face harassment and put-downs because they are women.
>
> (Bayton 1997: 46)

Globally, women are generally bombarded with images and constructions of femininity, much in the way that masculinity is defined by a series of traits and activities; these unwritten constructions must be confronted by women who are keen to break into their local scenes. Women who do favour electric guitar-driven music likely grew up seeing nothing but images of men who were afforded privileges and entitlements that patriarchy has granted them. Women also have few representations of themselves as guitar heroes. Most, throughout my discourse with women in Africa, simply did not see themselves represented as capable of performing the guitar, or any other instrument associated with rock or metal for that matter, and have likely been told that a woman simply did not have the skills to perform the guitar at a level of virtuosity. But this has certainly not deterred women from entering this treasured masculine space.

Cape Town-based guitar virtuoso Robyn Ferguson says she does not feel that the scene's masculine presence has fully deterred her determination, but there are the occasional antagonists. Instead of allowing the little vitriol she receives to hamper her work ethic, she has used this energy to serve as a 'learning curve of knowing when to stand firm', because, music is her way of 'expressing absolutely anything' (Ferguson 2020: n.pag.). For her, it is more than just seeing women performing in metal, it is about providing a space where creative people are inspired and encouraged to pursue their creativity (Ferguson 2020; see Figure 4.7).

Masculinity is a performance being done through any variety of provocative ways which exemplify the fragility of masculine behaviour because, as Judith Butler explains, gender is unstable, thus in constant defense and produced as 'a stylized repetition of facts' (Butler 1990: 140). Gabby Riches posits: 'The processes of exclusion or marginalization of women, and other minority groups, within heavy metal can be understood as mechanisms that work to ensure masculinity, whiteness and heterosexuality remain culturally and socially intelligible modes of metal' (Riches 2015: 268). Provided that masculinity is a performance, women in

FIGURE 4.7: Cape Town's Robyn Ferguson performing live at the Metal4Africa Summerfest in 2019. Photo copyright David Devo Oosthuizen – Devographic Music Agency.

the metal scene can shape how the genre is not only viewed, but also advanced. And, South Africa's scene has benefited greatly from the arrival of women who are redrafting the image of heavy metal to a generation that has greatly been in need of a clear definition of how to define who they are.

Women in the South African scene have enhanced the national heavy metal profile, whether as journalists, promoters, publicists or performers. Though women have not hesitated in expressing frustration with the masculine disdain that they feel has hampered their accomplishments and disrespected their work ethic, they understand quite well that women need to not only be fully integrated into the scene but also fully respected if the South African metal scene is to continue to grow. Sashquita Northey, a South African metal promoter and band manager says that women in the scene are no longer hampered by barriers nor challenged by their contributions:

I would not say that there are any clear barriers toward women today. Sure, in the past female groups were considered a novelty, but I think in South Africa the females that we do have who are on stage are actually quite revered and hailed within the South African context. They're well respected and liked amongst the community.

(Northey 2020: n.pag.)

Debbie Epstein suggests that South Africa's era of political transformation marked a change that could 'open up the possibility for those discourses which are usually marginalized to gain leverage' (1998: 50). Adding, there is the possibility of patriarchy and racism taking root again in South Africa (Epstein 1998: 50). Epstein feels that a 'revolution in masculinity' (1998: 51) can define healthy dialogues moving forward. In this void it is possible for a subculture to take hold of this conversation, understanding that the identity that participants maintain outside of the subculture's space would remain secondary while occupying primary subcultural spaces. This duality would signify that even participants outside of the traditional metal rubric are on equal footing when in the metal scene, whether as participants or as performers; it is their contributions to the metal scene that will be what is measured.

The global metal subculture faces the challenge of blurring gender, race and social classes. However, varying factors define why metal can be a 'safe' place. There is the reality that the South African heavy metal scene exits in a nation with a severe political and cultural hangover. As Martens says, this history has shaped the perception of how those from outside this genre's traditional rubrics are seen. 'Although we might be able to frequent the same spaces now, true integration, free of stereotyping, and unequal power relations just feels like a pipe-dream sometimes' (Martens 2019: n.pag.). But with the metal scene's profile increasing in the nation, things have begun to look up for potential participants.

Early performers in the South African rock and metal scene crafted their performances around masculinity to reaffirm the status quo because their lives depended on it. It was not until the late 1980s that the musicians began to understand that a status quo could be challenged more critically, notably with the arrival of the *Voëlvry* movement.

Saliently, South Africans who have embraced heavy metal as their identity have done so because they are drawn to this subculture's sense of community. The bond of community is what held together the scene in the face of the authoritarian state and is what is bringing down the barriers of this era. Communal identity is not national identity, it is a shared identity with those who have the same interests, and one of the more remarkable aspects of metal fandom is its ability to highlight a commonality. Heavy metal's lasting impact has more to do with its communal camaraderie than it does the music's accessibility. This is because the genre's response to 'cultural marginalization', and its participant's sense of ostracizing from the greater ills of society – whether in Western or non-Western settings – whether from the dictations of religious burdens, consumer driven aspirations, sexism, racism and economic inequalities, has allowed the subculture to create a community in which 'social problems are solved' (Riches 2011: 323).

With apartheid's end, the transition away from an authoritarian regime likely benefited participants in metal scenes by having a community of their own to tend to (Varas-Díaz et al. 2015: 91), thus possessing the attributes that build trust in a society: shared values, mutual identification and interaction as well as solidarity (Weinstein 2016: 10). Fan participation is contingent on the willingness to embrace this music and the identity that comes with their interaction within the subculture. Metal fandom has constructed a borderless identity precisely because of metal fan's alacrity to participate under a rubric of a shared identities, which in a diverse nation needs to exist without racial and gender prejudices. Without the burdens of an authoritarian government peeking over the shoulders of its citizenry, a fully welcoming and open metal scene would validate the national metal scene as the most viable metal scene in the African continent for generations.

Conclusion

South Africa's political transition brought along a new hope for the continent in a manner that came to symbolize a peaceful transition between disparate ideologies. Given that its history is tumultuous and divisive, it is not easy to grasp how a nation has been able to successfully transition from one of horror into one of promise. Historian and scholar Richard Dowden describes the South African transition as a 'miracle', one that was 'aspirational as well as protective, aiming to encourage the best in human beings while curbing their darker tendencies' (2009: 414).

It must be stated, and rather emphatically, that the modern South Africa is far from perfect, whether politically or socially. If there are any concerns about post-apartheid South Africa it is that the nation has seemingly transitioned from a one-party state ruled by the NP to another one-party state governed by the African National Congress (ANC). Since Mandela's historic election, his ANC party has been the only political party in control, and likely will remain so for quite some time.

White cynicism has been drawn towards false perceptions of inept leadership and graft in constant motion. However, cynicism does not allow for a clearer view of what is right in front of them. Though the ANC is less than perfect, they will not incriminate me for typing critical passages that reflect the ineptitude of their party and individual leaders. Journalists enjoy the freedom to work. Where under the rule of the NP, political dissidents were disappeared, political opposites today debate in public forums. And, notably, artists can speak loudly about the country and world as they see fit. Saliently, leadership in the country has strongly adhered to the words and merit of their democratic constitution. If anything is hurting the national psyche today it is that South Africa has been plagued by cynicism. This cynicism was fueled by the notion that the ANC would usher in a failed state, or a form of armed retaliation against the nation's Whites. None of this has come to fruition.

South African metal fans have realized the capabilities that exist within their community to push a new identity and nation forward because of the dialogue that heavy metal has to engage in has chosen to chase this cynicism away. Whereas metal musicians in previous decades were unable to reach beyond a base that reflected who they were, fans and musicians today are able to embrace the periphery that was once off limits. Furthermore, women have also been able to chip away at patriarchy that once directed them away from participating in the scene. Metal fans understand what is possible because they are quite aware of what this scene already endured.

They have identified with a subculture that has pushed away the cynicism that informed their predecessors, instead choosing to have a constructive dialogue about their nation's future through heavy metal music. Rare are the occasions that South Africans of various social strata have been able to come together, and unbeknownst to many in the nation the heavy metal scene has been bridging economic and racial divides far more efficaciously than any other form of music in the country.

5

Kenyan Dreams, Nairobi Nights: Heavy Metal and Hope in the Post-authoritarian Kenya

The third floor of a billiard hall known as the Crooked Q was decades removed from its last paint job. The lights were only working because of the maintenance done in the preparation for this evening. Toilets, however, were not. There was no running water to speak of on this floor. There also existed a sizable hole where there should have been a complete back wall. In its place, though, was a sheet of plastic, cracking and smacking at the slightest breeze.

Tonight this room served as nostalgia for someone who came of age attending DIY hardcore/punk shows in 'hole-in-the-wall' venues across central Pennsylvania. Though I do not think any of the rooms I moshed in during my teenage years actually had a hole in the wall, something about being here, on this night, brought a slight smile to me amidst my life-long aversion to overly crowded rooms.

For the assembled crowd, who had gathered from various corners of Kenya and a few other countries in the region, none of these details on this late September night seemed to matter. This night was too special to worry about how any foreign visitors thought about this space, this city or this country. All eyes were faced-forward towards the busy stage with eager anticipation. Just a few more smacks of the bass drum from the drummer, a quick vocal check from the vocalist, and a few more strums from the guitarist – now we were set! The lights went dim, the guitars came up and the crowd – mostly in their early 20s – began to roar in unison with the movement of their bodies. This is the moment they had been waiting for – the second-ever Nairobi Metal Festival (see Figure 5.1).

The Nairobi Metal Festival marked a return to Kenya for me. Five years prior, I had embedded myself within the rock and metal scene, a trip that exposed me to the conversations that Kenyan metal fans were having about their ethnic identity (Banchs 2016b). Throughout my first stint of fieldwork, I never made the connection that this was perhaps an inherent vestige of the nation's colonial past. Also, little did I know how some of the musicians were affected by a lot of the pressure

FIGURE 5.1: Tickets to the 2019 Nairobi Metal Festival. Photo by the author.

that the post-colonial identity left upon their existence considering they were a grandparent's generation removed from the end of colonial rule.

What follows in this chapter is a dialogue that will track the collision of the nation's political history with its current rock and heavy metal scene, one that is composed of the generation born mainly in the mid 90s. This generation has come into adulthood in a nation whose post-colonial economics are under the increasing influence of a new power in China, whose mark is evident upon venturing into the capital's business district. Here, the ever-expanding highway network snakes past the updated skyline taking shape in the city's Upperhill District, which has blossomed into a formidable cliche of pencil-tipped skyscrapers and tawdry oval-shaped edifices that resembled lipstick tubes, as well as any number of building with the word 'Tower' in them – encased in reflective windows by day, while broadcasting gaudy lighting by night. Nairobi is a palimpsest, a modern city being constructed right over the city built by the colonial government decades prior.

This chapter will also veer away from discussing metal in order to discuss Kenya's colonial era and postcolonial music history in order to better establish the context in which musicians in the country operate today. Rock and metal play a small part in the nation's overall musical picture because musically Kenya is as diverse a nation as any country in Africa. And, the country's musicians have long played a role in distracting citizenry from the ills that surrounded them, whether it was British rule or the postcolonial leaders that took their cues from their colonial masters. I have chosen to also discuss non-metal music in the colonial and post-colonial era because it was impossible to ignore how important these musical contributions are, in light of the obstacles that those musicians had to kick down in order to provide the musical infrastructure that is enjoyed by many today.

Much of the attention I will pay to the music that came before metal is done in order to establish how heavy metal and rock fits into Kenya's vast musical landscape. Further, this chapter will discuss the conversations being had by metal and rock musicians in the country today regarding their identity and the ethnic cleavages that generations of Kenyans have been told they had to embrace instead of abandon. How has colonialism impacted this generation? And, why is this important?

To start with...

Heavy metal in Kenya finds its origins among the millennial generation. I define millennial here as the generation that has come into adulthood during the turn of the century. This is the generation that has straddled both the pre- and post-internet life and, in the case of Kenya, this is the generation that straddled the era of the draconian rule of Daniel arap Moi, whose leadership came to an end in 2002.

I have previously detailed the genesis of the Kenyan metal scene in my book *Heavy Metal Africa: Life, Passion and Heavy Metal in the Forgotten Continent* (Banchs 2016a). In that book, I write about Xenostate (his preferred name in which to be quoted), a Kenyan born to American parents whose affinity for the American wave of grunge in the mid 90s inspired him to not only form his own band but also to share this music with those he knew. During our interview, Xenostate explained that his interest in this style of music came while in high school through his interactions with the son of a European ambassador, TK,[38] who came to Kenya with hundreds of CDs: 'Nuclear Blast stuff. Nirvana. Whatever was playing on the radio in the states is what we heard [...] he really kick-started everything [*sic*] off' (Xenostate 2013: n.pag.). He explains that previous to this, rock or metal was virtually non-existent to him – stagnant. It was after meeting TK and being introduced to this type of music that Xenostate made the transition from consumer to a performer, forming his first band Impish in 2001, which evolved into his second band, Class Suicide, featuring many of the same members.

Acting as a catalyst Xenostate explains that most of the members of these early bands also bounced between acts as a way of not only learning their craft but also combining their resources and acumen:

Us and a couple of bands in 2001 bonded together and bought equipment. I assembled whatever equipment I could from the States and brought it back for the purpose of recording hardcore. We had some pretty good amps, but it was really do it yourself. If we didn't bring it from the States, you were having to assemble yourself. I found a drum set at my high school that was going to be thrown away; I had to weld my own cymbal stands. But we wanted to have something we could put out there. We wanted to have a compilation of all our bands, to take it to the next level.

(Xenostate 2013: n.pag.)

On his own impetus, Xenostate also began recording his band and promoting performances of local bands. Though he left to attend university in the United States, he would return home as often as possible during breaks. During these breaks, he would organize shows along with a few others, recalling, 'the difficulty was getting people to come to the shows' (Banchs 2016a: 139).

Often told that this type of music would not fare very well in Kenya, as it was a style that had not been widely exposed in the country, the response to Class Suicide performances soared beyond his expectations – he describes it as 'massive' – as he and his bandmates' confidence soared as a result (Banchs 2016a: 139). After that he says: 'It took on a life on its own. From that point I was really inspired' (Xenostate 2013: n.pag.).

Xenostate's Class Suicide bandmate, Talal Cocker, remembers this era with fondness as it marked a period where they were not only learning about this type of music, but they were also learning about the culture of the music they were performing, notably the 'do-it-yourself' (DIY) mentality that is indicative of punk and hardcore scenes worldwide. It was Cocker who approached the marketing of this nascent scene by designing posters, fanzines, stickers and stencils while learning as they went (see Figure 5.2). The members of Class Suicide were both performers and students of the scene, keeping their passion for the genre alive as well as their band during their terms abroad as a few of them had enrolled in universities outside of Kenya. As Cockar says, he used his time as a student abroad to also absorb what he could of his newfound love:

I learned about making zines and DIY art from folks in the punk scene in the US while I was in university. Every time we came home, we brought new music and ideas with us and shared them with our little group of friends. Most people didn't understand what we were doing, and we often got laughed at or were given disgusted looks. In a way, it kind of fueled our fire and we became so defiantly DIY despite some people telling us to get sponsors for the shows. We didn't want anyone to tell us what music to play, how to play it, where to play it, what to look like or what our flyers should look like.

(2019: n.pag.)

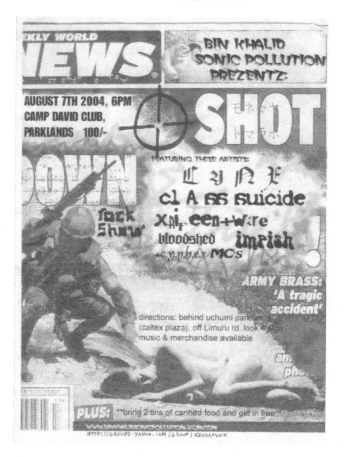

FIGURE 5.2: 2004 flyer featuring Class Suicide. Courtesy of Xenostate.

Cockar also helped form the Wiyathi Collective – 'freedom' in Kikuyu – a punk-minded collaboration that existed with the objective of organizing events, publishing their own zine and providing safe spaces for those gaining an interest in this type of music (see Figure 5.3). These were spaces that were intolerant of racism and homophobia. 'I hope it was seen as a way to create safe spaces for Queer or Trans, at least that was our intention', (Cockar 2020: n.pag.). Though, it should be noted that shows were not held in one set location. Concerts were often shuffled around Nairobi and hosted in venues that allowed these types of bands to perform for the night.

This period in Nairobi's rock and metal nascence was marked by bands such as Rock of Ages, who formed as a church band and were performing rock covers in the mid 90s before writing original material. Other acts that were active and

FIGURE 5.3: Wiyathi Collective zines (n.d.). Photo Courtesy of Talal Cockar.

performing original material during this time included Bloodshed, Navarone, Fireproof, M2O, Creeping Wire and Point of Vertigo, as well as the earliest incarnation of Last Year's Tragedy. Some of these bands, including the latter, formed by way of university introductions as students in the late 90s, as they 'particularly listened to grunge, punk and heavy metal' (Knopke 2019: 188).

Simultaneously, as this nascent musical culture was being embraced and expressed artistically, this era also marked a change for the nation politically: their government was undergoing a political transformation in 2002, marking the first time Kenya would experience a successful democratic transition since the end of their colonial era. Rock and heavy metal leapt into the Kenyan landscape at a time when the nation was ready to shed its vestigial skin of colonialism and embrace the possibilities of living in a successful democracy.

The presidential elections held on 27 December 2002 in Kenya would mark the end for the long-time president Daniel arap Moi, who had presided over the country since 1978. Only Kenya's second president since independence in 1963, Moi was constitutionally barred from running. Though his Kenyan African National Union (KANU) party – the only political party to control the nation since independence – would have a ballot representative in Uhuru Kenyatta (Astill 2002), Kenya was ready for a change.

The elections were won by the National Rainbow Coalition (NARC), which was seen to mark a 'triumph in ethnic pluralism and national rejuvenation'

(Kagwanja 2005: 51). The victorious Mwai Kibaki was greeted by an emotional crowd, to the point of chanting 'Kibaki! He has beaten Moi!', during his swearing-in ceremony, while simultaneously lobbing clumps of mud towards their outgoing leader (Bond 2002: n.pag.).

Garnering a pat on the back from international observers who felt that Kenya was finally realizing its democratic potential, many citizens felt the tides of transparency and justice were not going to swing their way. Many citizens were bracing for a carbon copy of the status quo: graft, ethnic polarization and a greater disparity between economic classes. This is the state in which the early rock and metal bands of Kenya found their impetus: A country bound between uncertainty and promise.

A long time comin'

Kenya came to the African map in the same way most African colonial possessions did, by way of the *Berlin Conference* of West Africa. This conference marked the apogee of the Scramble for Africa, which occurred primarily in the second half of the 1800s and was a volleying of greed that witnessed Western European states vying for resources and land in the continent in order to build their wealth. Adventurous and obsequious explorers travelled the continent lining up land and prospects for their nations, staking claims as they walked, setting up this 'scramble'. As historian Lawrence James writes: 'Brazen opportunism and pugnacity were vital qualities for the pathfinders of empire' (2017: 92).

Held during the winter of 1884–85, the *Berlin Conference* of West Africa was where European powers carved the continent for themselves. Though Russia and the United States sent representatives, both nations abstained from the process. Not one African representative was present in the room. The business of drawing Africa's new borders saw 'ministers and diplomats [lock] horns over claims and counterclaims and agreed compromises designed not to unduly hurt the *amour propre* of the powers involved' (James 2017: 90). As a result of German expanses over East Africa, the British government made a deal with Germany for recognition over what is today Uganda, Kenya and Zanzibar in exchange for Tanzania and an island in the North Sea, Heligoland.

For the British, who already controlled Egypt, the motive was simple: control the source and flow of the Nile River. The British 'wanted to protect the upper reaches of the river, to keep other European powers out of Uganda and Sudan, and to carefully safeguard all of the possible approaches to the White Nile' (Rotberg 1965: 274).

In order to keep the costs of running a colony low, the British established a charter company 'along the lines of the old, profitable East India Company' (Rotberg 1965: 273), giving birth to the British East Africa Company in 1888. British aristocracy agreed this was the best path forward as it would 'maintain and extend British influence [...] to develop British trade, and to deal in a practical manner with the Slave Trade' (Coupland 1939: 427). The company would be turned over to the British government in 1895.

Under colonial rule, Kenya followed much of the cannon scripted around the continent: Land was seized without consent or fair compensation and handed to 'settlers' – British expats who were encouraged to move to the new African colonies. In turn, the populations of those whose ancestors took the first footsteps of humanity were pushed to the side, stamped out of the land that was synched to their existence. During the colonial era, Africa was a profit margin for European governments. British rule in Kenya, however, took an unexpected turn.

In October of 1952, a state of emergency was declared in Kenya as a group, dominated by members of the Kikuyu ethnic group known as the Kenya Land and Freedom Army (KLFA), who had grown suspicious of other Kikuyu's loyalty to the colonial government, had taken arms against their own. Known as the Mau Mau, the conflict that ensued was a direct result of land disputes. With the onset of the arrival of Whites from England, the government had allocated fertile land in an area that became known as the 'white highlands' in the Rift Valley province. In doing so the Maasai inhabitants were displaced in order to meet the labour demands needed to farm the land. Kikuyu peasants moved from the nearby Kikuyuland to work the farms. In exchange these 'squatters', as they were known (they paid their rent with labour), succeeded as independent producers of their own.

By the mid 1940s, of the one million Kikuyus in Kenya, one in every four lived in what was referred to as the 'White highlands'. However, directly after the Second World War, the demographics once again shifted in the region as 'some 8,000 white immigrants arrived in Kenya, escaping postwar austerity in Europe' (Meredith 2005: 82), thus forcing many of the Kikuyu squatters off of the leased lands to make room for the recent arrivals who were now only dependent on wage labourers.

Furthermore, the British government set aside a quarter of a million acres exclusively for former British ex-servicemen – noting that 100,000 Kenyans were also ex-servicemen who fought for the British in the East African Wars – leading many squatters to take up a resistance campaign. This 'squatters revolt' was the impetus of the Mau Mau.

The Mau Mau escalation would become one of the more devastating colonial wars in Africa. In total 3000 soldiers and police officers, 12,000 Mau Mau supporters (allegedly) and 1800 civilians were killed (Dowden 2009: 425). This conflict forced Britain to rethink its hold on Kenya as it contemplated loosening its colonial grip sooner than it had wished. Jomo Kenyatta, who was detained in 1961 as a suspected mastermind of the Mau Mau (he was not), was elected as Kenya's first prime minister shortly after independence on 1 June 1963.

'Trouble-makers, debauchees, and rebels'

The musical output that preceded the Second World War and continued into the end of the colonial era in Kenya has been remembered as one that allowed musicians in the country to set themselves apart with a voice of their own, voices that reflected an independent spirit and identity.

As a result of service to their colonial government in the Second World War and East African campaign, many musicians in Kenya began to play the music that was influenced by an instrument that many were noticing throughout their tours, including to Europe and Asia, and were returning with: the electric guitar. This post-war music was new and vivacious, possessing a fresh approach to the ubiquitous instrument as it would be marked by infusions of the traditional music of Kenya and East Africa. Examples of a Kenyan musical styling that was influencing electric guitar players in the nation include *Luhya* music or *Sukuti*. These two styles are identified by the rhythms of a traditional instrument known as the *litungu*, a seven-stringed lyre marked by its distinctive oval body (Wanyama 2019: 363) whose music and accompanying dance, *kamabeka* (a tradition of the Bukusu ethnic group) are marked by rhythmic strumming.

John Low, in an article titled 'A history of Kenyan guitar music: 1945–80' says that though guitar music existed in the country before the Second World War, the 'collective recall' insists that recordings and contributions from Kenya's guitarists of note took root in 1945 (1982: 17). These artists included Paul Machupa, Jumbe, Kataka and notably Fundi Konde, likely the first guitarist in East Africa to perform on an electric guitar (Ewens 2000).

Similar to what happened to European and American soldiers upon returning from war, Kenyan musicians were also plagued with post-war stresses that led to embattlements in their personal lives which many combatted with alcohol. Musicians who returned from the war[39] were not only combatting post-traumatic stress syndrome but also the lingering stress colonialism was wreaking on their mental health – heroes for the British, yet subjects in their own country. Musicians were desperate to find a sound that reflected their feelings, thus taking to performing a more rebellious and deviant form of music that seemed to best capture the sentiment of their post-war life. 'They were introducing sort of popular styles

[...] they were playing very much European styles, American sort of styles. Rock', says Nairobi-based journalist Bill Odidi (2019: n.pag.).

Viewed as 'trouble-makers, debauchees, and rebels' (Low 1982: 26) by both the traditional authorities and the colonial administration, John Low explains:

> Guitarists were part of a new order of things. As we have seen, some of the earliest Kenyan guitarists learned guitar from foreigners while fighting in the 2nd world war. Travel, meeting men from other countries, new ideas: these things broadened the minds of Kenyan soldiers—politicized them [...] Guitarists were amongst those who, returning to the country, had tasted, however briefly, a different style of life. Whole others bore suffering and poverty stoically, and respected customs, these young people were often disrespectful, impatient for change and better things. Not surprisingly, they often clashed with their families, the chiefs, the church, and the administration. Many guitarists told me that life has been very difficult for them.
>
> (1982: 26)

The music of this era was able to be documented by way of recording studios that were opening in Nairobi during the post-war era. Though not all of the musicians were able to achieve professional incomes, there were several artists whose names became ubiquitous by way of various recording studios, including Columbia Broadcasting Studio, which recorded an estimated 1000 records a month (Mwendwa 2019). However, two studios founded by British expats would come to shape the identity and sounds in the lead up to independence: Equator Records and His Majesty's Voice.

Settling in Kenya after the end of the Second World War, Charles Worrod invested in East African Records, a label he would sell before forming the Equator Sound Studios Limited in Nairobi in 1960 with the intention of marketing 'East African music for East Africans' (Odidi 2013a: n.pag.). The company did so well that musicians from the region seized any and every opportunity they could to record for Worrod, travelling to Nairobi for open auditions held on Saturdays. Those who left an impression 'would be recorded the next day' (Odidi 2013a: n.pag.).

The label also served as the home of The Equator Sound Band, Kenya's answer to the Wrecking Crew – an American group of studio musicians that recorded many of the best-known songs of their era. The Equator Sound Band's core included Fadhili William, Daudi Kabaka, Ugandan Charles Sonko and two Zambians, Nashil Pichen Kazembe and Peter Tsotsi Juma. Fadhili Williams would later find success as a songwriter and musician writing Kenya's first international hit in 1960, 'Malaika'.[40]

Another success from the studio was Daudi Kabaka's song '*Harambee Harambee*', (1965). The song became so cherished in Kenya that it is still revered and often referred to as Kenya's second national anthem. Driven by an electric guitar rhythm, '*Harambee Harambee*' is performed in the Swahili language and is largely influenced by the *kwela* style of music that Worrod was a fan of (see Allen 2019). With the intent of composing a song that could translate well to the newly independent nation, '*Harambee Harambee*' served as a unifying melody. Bill Odidi writes:

> National broadcaster, Voice of Kenya (VOK), used the recording of the song by the Kenya Army Band as the signature tune for its radio news for the next four decades. In his memoirs, Worrod, who died in South Africa in 2008, writes that he never earned a single cent in royalties from VOK because the Government said '*Harambee Harambee*' was a national song and did not deserve any payment.
>
> (Odidi 2013b: n.pag.)

Equator Sound's output not only provided a cherished musical catalogue but also invalidated the idea, held by many, that a Kenyan music industry would be impossible, as the success of the label locally and the manner in which the business was conducted paralleled the paradigm of Western labels. Kenyans were working and performing alongside a business model and musical infrastructure that rivalled any in the West.

Arriving in Kenya in the late 1930s to work as an air traffic controller, Peter Colmore also took an interest in the sounds he was hearing from local musicians, notably Fundi Konde (whose records Colmore would later produce) and Daniel Katuga, both of whom were members of the Kings African Rifles. With the British involvement in the Second World War, Colmore would have to wait to pursue his musical ambitions as he was called to serve as a captain in the East African Forces.

Upon returning, Colmore formed the eponymous Peter Colmore African Band with a friend, Ally Sykes. It was this platform that allowed Colmore to work with musicians that he enjoyed, notably the Congolese guitarists Jean-Bosco Mwenda and Edouard Masengo. With the national musical output taking a long pause as a result of the Mau Mau, Colmore engaged in producing music and commercial jingles for the BBC as well as a local record label, His Master's Voice Blue Label, before venturing out on his own to form High Fidelity Productions Ltd. in 1959 as the Mau Mau conflict was coming to an end (Kiereini 2018). Through the medium of commercial jingles, Colmore was able to extend the reach of traditional music to homes in urban and rural settings (Kiereini 2018).

Both Colmore and Worrod's record companies, the artists that recorded in those spaces, and the songs that were produced during this period served as the foundation for Kenya's musical possibilities and aspirations. 'The presence of this [helped] Kenyan people push a big rally factor around Kenyan identity', says Odidi (2019: n.pag.). The need to rely on Western music to entertain Kenyan ears was rivalled by local artists producing music with a local flair in more familiar languages with messages intended for local audiences. This formed a significant shift in Kenyan identity, especially as the nation was on the verge of independence: Music by Kenyans for Kenyans.

The 1970s and 80s era of music continued with its own musical legacies, yet without any contributions from rock and heavy metal, which was beginning to soar on radio and television dials in the West. In Kenya, artists such as Kelly Brown – dubbed the Michael Jackson of Kenya – Sal Davis, The Mighty Cavaliers and The Ashanti pushed through sounds that encompassed the soulful hooks of Motown and disco with the fusions of Afrobeat.

Lyrically, acts stepped away from the nation's politics, performing music that served to put people into nightclubs and away from rallies. This was also likely spurred by the political slip into authoritarianism under the rule of Daniel arap Moi, who maintained a tight grip on the nation. Recordings that aired on national airwaves were also being monitored for subversive content, a practice that was established by the colonial government.

Many songs of the Moi era were markedly romantic, gregarious simulacrums from the West – a step away from 'the trauma and tension of the colonial and Neo-independence movements' (Nyairo 2005: 34).

There were moments, however, that indicated that music served political purposes. As Peter Wafalu Wakesa explains, music in Kenya is political, serving to fill the role of 'exerting political pressure, spreading propaganda and reflectivity and moulding public opinion' (2004: 97). Wakesa notes that traditional music specifically has been shown as a useful form of expression in articulating political commentary:

> [As] songs specifically associated with the various facets of government are numerous among the particular ethnic groups within Kenya. However, although the earlier traditional songs are still being incorporated in commenting on aspects of the Kenyan political process, contemporary songs appear more direct and forthright in their statement on policy, goals and platforms than the older ones.
>
> (2004: 102)

In some cases throughout the nation's post-colonial history, there has been music produced that has been adapted as political, regardless of the artist's original intent. One such song in Kenya was Gidi Gidi Maji Maji's popular song *'Unbwogable'* ('I Am Unbeatable'). Released in September of 2002, the song was born out of a motivational chant between two performers, as Nyairo and Ogude posit: this was a reflection of a moment, one of 'pain, anger, dejection, near-despair, and in the midst of all these, their sheer determination, translate into an individual's struggle for space, for freedom from the pressures and disappointments of daily existence' (2005: 231). This song became a massive hit for the group only to be banned by the Moi government as it was interpreted as an indictment on his administration. Yet, and perhaps as a form of political courting, the opposition embraced the song, gracing 'nearly every gathering of the opposition parties and especially the campaign rallies of the NARC candidates' (Nyairo and Ogude 2005: 233).

Whereas music could ideally serve as a point of unity, this is an example where a song was used for political promotion, likely a result of the song's success in correlation with the campaign season – a desperate reach of validation by NARC, who later asked Gidi Gidi Maji Maji's producer Tedd Josiah to replace the ethnically Luo elements with aspects of various ethnic groups 'to give the song a broader national appeal while all along retaining "*Unbwogable's*" catchy, assertive and provocative chorus' (Nyairo and Ogude 2005: 240).

Innocence was not an attribute of all the music in a country that had just barely reached cruising altitude, as the weight of living within a structure that kept restrictive mechanisms within reach forced musicians into a corner that a few were able to navigate out of. Despite this, Kenyans were reveling in their sovereignty apropos of the despotic mechanisms of the Moi government that were hidden from sight, flaws that the next generation would not forgive. With Moi's term up, art was able to move in a different direction as the clouded level of fear was slowly disappearing.

Untying the ropes

The 2002 election was the catalyst for those in the nascent punk and metal scene to take their leap forward away from the underground. Metal, punk and rock musicians could now step out and perform songs that they felt best represented their Kenya, their lives and their history even if it was once unspeakable. Metal would address the ugliness of colonialism, the heartache of one-party rule, the frustrations of economic uncertainty and the melancholy that lingers throughout their daily lives. Of the bands whose performance at the Nairobi Metal Festival stood out for me was Petrika, a band that had formed in the years since my first visit, and whose sound was a quiet detachment from the metalcore that was dominating the scene. Their sound was dark, clouded in mystery, engulfed in a melancholy rooted alongside their post-punk, grunge influences. Their performance that evening was less than desirable, however, as their rehearsal schedule did not resemble that of a professional band, nor did they own any of their own equipment.[41] Bands in Nairobi, for the most part, had to use equipment that was already in the rehearsal spaces they rented, which was only undertaken in anticipation of a concert. Petrika, being a new band, took to the stage in what more closely resembled a rehearsal than a performance. I was, however, taken by their vocalist's disposition, one that was reserved yet honest, a performer that did not shy away from telling the audience what each song was about – nihilism, death and apathy, a cathartic release from the darkness that he feels encases his life.

A timorous presence, Petrika's vocalist Brian Saibore explains that metal, to him, is therapeutic as it helps express those dark emotions that plague him (see Figure 5.4). It helps him discuss the every day, the feelings of isolation and sadness that are, in his view, prevalent in the metal scene and a reason why he feels there

FIGURE 5.4: Petrika's Brian Saibore performing at the 2019 Nairobi Metal Festival. Photo by Portia T. Muigai.

is a strong community around a metal show (Saibore 2019). Metal has found itself in Kenya because this a form of music that the fans have discovered to best reflect their lives, one that encapsulates who they are right now. 'When you listen to your own kind of music, there is so much more you can do with that', says Saibore (2019: n.pag.).

During our conversation, I wondered why he felt that there was constant darkness hovering over the local metal scene when the jubilation experienced a few days before during the festival stood in contrast to his words. He explained that this was because metal fans had found a way of pulling themselves away from the 'system' – referring to British colonialism – through music: 'We are all victims [...] They used those people who are weaker than them to be more powerful', he says (Saibore 2019: n.pag.). The incredibly reserved frontman sat with his locked hands resting in front of his tall frame before discussing his views on his nation's past with quiet sincerity. His eyes fixed on the floor throughout most of our interview. Much of his words were a response to how this music had made him feel and what performing meant to him. However, his demeanour and body position shifted when we switched course to discussing British colonial rule, the post-colonial politics in Kenya and whether or not this music was a reaction not only to their political history but also a response to colonialism.

> There are many subcultures that can pull a person out of this system and metal is one of them. Metalheads don't care for modern music that is readily fed to the masses by the radio. They don't care for trends. All they need is a black trouser, band merch and a leather jacket. They depend very little on the government, church or society's approval to get closure. There is a very huge universe outside this tiny box that the system has created. And the metalhead knows this, and is always exploring this world that is referred to as evil.
>
> (Saibore 2019: n.pag.)

Like Saibore, others too, felt that rock and metal were the perfect response to post-colonial realities not only because of the camaraderie and community that has formed around the scene but also because this type of music allows for dialogue around past and present political and social issues. The 'system' that Saibore referred to is a construction: a modern nation built in the image of a Western government, constructing ethnic identities and hierarchy, wrapping all of this into a capitalist-driven business model that Kenyans were promised would get them out of poverty. The post-colonial experience has seemingly failed, and metal musicians felt they could confront the status quo.

Daniel 'Bizarro' Mwangi, the vocalist of metalcore act Aphasia, shared that metal bands and fans in Nairobi are working together because, in his view, metal in Kenya is a response to colonialism: 'A people breaking themselves free of those chains of colonialism and having a voice of their own through it [...] we are still blinded by these colonies who still make us believe we need them even for progress', he says (Mwangi 2019: n.pag.), noting that economically, the British have yet to let go of what once was theirs.

But how did the political situation affect the rock and metal scene? For the rock and metal community, these political appropriations did not suit their personal interests. In Kenya metal has acted as a gateway to Western avenues away from scripted traditional identity into a more global cosmopolitanism (see Banchs 2016b), one in which the music could be used to reflect their views on issues in a more emotional manner, less so overtly political. DJ Switch, a local metal/rock DJ, posits that 'rock in Kenya has never been politically motivated. Actually, most rockers/metal heads are apathetic when it comes to politics in general' (Switch 2019: n.pag.), and noting that there perhaps was a greater correlation with the arrival of the internet[42] and the spread of metal and rock within the country. Mayer and Timberlake have also posited through a quantitative study that Kenya,[43] as a country without a strong history of metal, likely benefited from the rise of the internet as a strong factor for cultural diffusion (2014: 42).

For some, though, the rock and metal scene has always been affected by the nation's politics. As mentioned earlier, Talal Cockar recalls having difficulty in promoting early punk shows, featuring bands and zines whose music and message was rooted in anarchism and anti-fascism because the Moi government always seemed to be watching. Police would directly threaten his father (a noted business owner in Nairobi), insisting that they would do harm to his family if he did not stop his 'activism' (Cockar 2020: n.pag.), after he began to distribute leaflets on the ideals of Anarchism around Nairobi and formed a political discussion group at the National Theater. These threats were visible reminders that the early punk and metal scene was going to have difficulty during the Moi era (Cockar 2019).

Apropos of DJ Switch's sentiment, it is more than likely that this form of music took on a different meaning to its players and participants as a direct result of the nation's social reconstruction that occurred after the transitional election. Mayer and Timberlake have indicated that nations with strong democratic institutions and stronger economic integration are generally more than likely to produce more rock and metal acts than nations with higher per capita incomes (Mayer and Timberlake 2014: 41). The structure of a thriving scene that allows its participants to access metal's global network is better facilitated in more liberal governments, as it would be by those who come from nations that enjoy access to global connectivities, including suitable and open internet access, which has greatly shaped the ability to accumulate heavy metal's economic capital (Kahn-Harris 2011: 2007).

For aspiring musicians discovering this type of music during the Moi era, the untying of the tension that came with the 2002 elections greatly assisted in the formation of the metal scene as the easing of a one-party state allowed for a greater engagement with a new fanbase, the element of a hovering eye having been largely eliminated. Cockar concurs that the political tides shifted open the possibility for this music to exist:

> There was a general sense that we were on the brink of a major change after more than twenty years of Moi's presidency and we saw a more emboldened press, more open political discourse. I don't think that necessarily prompted us to start doing all of this but it's possible that the changing political tides helped us feel that we could be more open about our political opinions and social discourse.
>
> (2019: n.pag.)

One act in the Kenyan scene whose music has reflected this new dialogue well is Crystal Axis, a punk band that has chosen to confront the horror of Africa and Kenya's past. The band formed in 2008 when the members were all teenagers, but with varying intervals of hiatuses in between (most of the members attended universities outside of Kenya) it was not until 2017 that the band formally reintroduced themselves. The following year, they released their breakout song, 'Leopold', (Crystal Axis 2018) which discusses European colonialism in the Congo through the horrendous atrocities committed by the former Belgian ruler King Leopold. The track, along with its accompanying lyric video, garnered attention outside of Kenya. The band's guitarist, Djae Aroni, says[44] this song was their way of finally being able to address the past, to shift the conversation of colonialism towards a greater African perspective, not just a Kenyan one.

King Leopold's rule in the neighbouring Congo, known today as the Democratic Republic of Congo, was the catalyst of Europe's scramble that shaped the continent for the worse, and led to the *Berlin Conference* of West Africa. Crystal Axis' lyrics[45] discuss the practice in which Leopold's officers would chop off a local Congolese hand at random for the sake of asserting control over the 'brutes and savages'; the Belgians, in turn, maintained a posture of sagacity in the years since Leopold's rule (see Hochschild 1998). In the song, the band performs:

I'm spinning into control,
Gold is food for the soul.
I stole and plundered your own,
I got you stuck in my hold! [...]
I'm going to eat you alive,
Skin and bones it's suppertime,

A shop of horrors sublime,
History says I'm alright!
I'm the king and it's all mine,
Under Force Publique and Christ,
Your hands are mine tonight,
Fingers up one time!

(Crystal Axis 2018)

Crystal Axis, as Africans, are not oblivious to the Western narrative of history and have asserted their perspective on a matter that they felt needed to be clarified, since a narrative of false and negative perceptions has mired the continent since independence. Aroni describes their music as an attitude that informs the listeners of what to expect thematically more so than a sound; he describes their music as the emancipation of mental slavery from the confines of conventional or traditional thoughts and beliefs, which he indicates is a strong Western dialogue that continues to shape African narratives:

Schools all over the world teach about Hitler and other horrors faced in Europe, but seldom talk about the atrocities committed against Africans and other people of colour. It became evident to us that as Africans, we have to tell our own stories and create dialogue amongst ourselves. We believe that it's our duty as musicians to address these issues through our art.

The topic of European colonialism within Africa, and the world over, is something that has not been addressed properly over the years. In fact, a lot of the times it gets swept under the rug and ignored by many Westerners. Earlier this year [2017] a French politician[46] had the audacity to describe colonialism as a 'mere exchanging of culture'. Pillaging and robbing African lands while simultaneously enslaving and killing the population is not a sharing of culture, and it is a shame that such an important topic is waved away. Our music will touch on this issue and other issues affecting Africans and people of colour.

(Aroni[47] 2017: n.pag.)

Crystal Axis' follow up to 'Leopold' further continued their narrative of addressing issues from the nation's past that Kenyans had long avoided. Released in 2019, 'Nyayo House' highlights one of the more tumultuous aspects of the Moi era, his penchant for detaining, torturing and, in some cases, disappearing political rivals, journalists and scholars – all rumoured to be political dissidents – in the basement detention facility of a 27-floor skyscraper located in Nairobi's city centre. This building became the centre of a struggle for a multi-party state, which would mark the end of the Moi regime. In the song, Crystal Axis sings:

Take my license, steal my soul,
Throw me in a cold, dark hole.
13 doors all painted red,
They say it never existed, 'Baba[48], it's all in your head'.

(Crystal Axis 2019)

Moi's intimidating and secret police was also addressed by metalcore act Irony Destroyed with their 2019 song 'Najiskia Kuua Tena' ('I feel the urge to kill again'), a song performed in Sheng,[49] a pidgin variation of Swahili. Whether or not all bands are choosing to engage with the country's political history, there are other messages that are being relayed because of the challenges of living in a nation that is struggling to find a post-colonial identity, those of personal identity.

2007: March from the underground

One moment that presented itself as a challenge to Kenyans' identity, as well as a point of dialogue for today's rock and metal scene, was the violence that was spurred as a result of the 2007 election, the second since the end of Moi's rule. Instead of being noted as another landmark step away from authoritarianism, this election would be remembered for its callous and apathetic response from the political figures at the centre of the elections as a result of the violent aftermath the elections left, a wound that is still infecting the nation.

Raila Odinga and Mwai Kibaki both agreed to form the NARC coalition that defeated Moi's KADU party in the 2002 elections. After Kibaki emerged victoriously, the two entered a Memorandum of Understanding that would have created a Prime Minister post for Odinga, with Kibaki assuming more power under the Presidency. Kibaki backed off his promise, eventually forming his own political party. Five years later Odinga's Orange Democratic Movement (ODM) faced off against the incumbent Kibaki, who was then representing his newly founded Party of National Unity (PNU).

That December, with the eyes of the world's observers keenly awaiting the election winner, Kibaki announced he had emerged victorious without the results having been counted in full. Odinga, rebutting Kibaki's claims, asked for a recount. Before any of this could occur, violence would erupt between ethnic groups. Much of the unrest 'took the shape of an ethnic conflict' between the Kikuyu, Embu and Meru groups that backed Kibaki and the Luo and Kalenjin that supported Odinga (Harneit-Sievers and Peters 2008: 133). It is estimated that more than 1500 people were killed, 'mainly in the Rift Valley, Nyanza Province and Nairobi. At least 350,000 people were evicted from their homes' (Harneit-Sievers and Peters 2008: 133).

This was violence spurred by ethnic cleavages and exploited by politicians years after the end of the colonial 'divide and rule' ethos. This rhetoric of ethnicity was dangerous and continues to plague the nation by way of continual stereotypes and generalizations based on others' appearances and names. A few generations removed from the colonial era, Kenyans were still being raised to adhere to the colonialists' image (see Ranger 1992). The British had failed to create a national identity, instead of creating a system of hierarchy that rewarded Kenyans based on perceived differences and positions defined by labour. Thus, political parties would evolve to be centred around ethnicity. 'Given the absence of a solid foundation for national political organization, the already entrenched nature of regional [tribal] associations was bound to be the predominant feature of political organizations' (Ajulu 2002: 257).

The likely cause of this ethnic polarization is a sense of hopelessness that has remained in the independence era. As Gabrielle Lynch asserts:

> Feelings of marginalization can lead community leaders to assert their difference to their neighbours, and in some cases to forge new alliances to strengthen their voice. The argument, therefore, unfolds thus: we cannot expect politician X to fight for, protect and promote our interests because we are not of his community.
>
> (2006: 61)

These differences were summed up with two words I had never heard put together until I interviewed David Mburu, vocalist of the country's most recognizable metal act, Last Year's Tragedy, during my first trip to Kenya: 'We have to put in mind that we are culture-raised' (Banchs 2016a: 146), he lamented. He adds that the previous generation, his parents' generation, brought him up with this mindset – 'culture raised' – in which you were expected to adhere strictly to the norms of your culture, and continue to build on the traditions established by their ancestors. This was merely a trick by the colonial government to ensure that they could maintain a semblance of control by dividing Kenyans based on culture. During my follow-up trip, those two words were being repeated when asked if the British were clever colonizers: 'I was raised to be cultural', says Saibore (2019: n.pag.). This idea of being culturally raised, in his view, was a direct result of Britain's colonial legacy.

Today, Kenya is home to dozens of ethnic groups and a population that speaks any one of more than three dozen languages. While no ethnic group dominates, a 2019 survey estimate reveals the larger groups include Kikuyu[50] Luhya, Kalenjin and Luo (CIA 2020). Most of the discourses on superiority versus inferiority between ethnic groups, created by the British system of 'divide and rule' are still well placed inside of the mind of the nation's ruling classes, who took their cues from the colonial government, which encouraged ethnic thought. Kenyans are swimming in a colonial-tainted pool, and the metal scene has chosen to navigate the spaces above the water.

Formed shortly after the political transition of 2002, Last Year's Tragedy has used their music to reflect on the violence that afflicted their country by penning various songs on the matter, including 'Challenge Accepted' (2013a) and 'March From the Underground' (2013b). Given their status as Kenya's most popular metal act, it came as no surprise that they were the chosen headliners for the first night of the Nairobi Metal Fest. The band has remained a solid presence since their arrival at the scene. The seven-piece has meant so much to fans in the nation, as their songs have become anthems for an audience that was eager to express their life in this country, notably 'March From the Underground', which culminated with a roomful shouting in unison that evening:

We're not looking back,
We're moving forward now,
Hold on, don't let go,
We'll all see this through.

(Last Year's Tragedy 2013b)

The song concludes with an even more powerful refrain that spilled onto the street three floors below:

March on, March on!

(Last Year's Tragedy 2013b)

The power of these moments is never lost on any music fan. For metal fans, these moments carry a bit more weight. These are not songs broadcast on local radio. These are not anthems that have been passed on to them by their parents. These are songs they discovered on their own, created by circumstance they never asked for, reflecting how they feel and who they are. Aphasia's Mwangi (see Figure 5.5), who was one of the voices pressed up front, screaming along during Last Year's Tragedy's set, says this is why he was personally able to connect to this type of music.

Metal has absolutely changed my view of the world, as it's not just a form of entertainment for me but has also been a tool that speaks on the atrocities around us in

138

FIGURE 5.5: Aphasia's Daniel Mwangi performing at the 2019 Nairobi Metal Festival. Photo by the author.

black and white. One that many people are scared to talk about especially in this very politically-driven side of the region.

(Mwangi 2019: n.pag.)

'March From the Underground' has become this anthem for Last Year's Tragedy and for those who have taken this band to heart. 'March on' continues to serve as the band's unofficial rally cry, which is revisited on their 2020 single 'Pounds For Flesh':

All I know is what I'm made of when I'm marching from the underground,
All is see is where we come from we learnt our lessons that hard way.

(Last Year's Tragedy 2020)

Last Year's Tragedy (see Figure 5.6) also challenged the post-election violence through political perspectives in their song 'Tribute to Anarchy' (Last Year's Tragedy 2011a). The song implicates the nation's leadership for their lack of accountability before, during and in the aftermath of the violence, even hinting in the press release for the song that a few politicians likely encouraged the violence,[51] stating 'the people in power who could have stopped the fighting but didn't, who

FIGURE 5.6: Last Year's Tragedy stealing the show at the 2019 Nairobi Metal Festival. Photo by the author.

could have saved lives but didn't, who could have united our nation but caused it to split' (Last Year's Tragedy 2011b: n.pag.):

> Forgiveness.
> Battle lines, Where all is lost,
> That's where our story begins,
> It's hard to forget and forgive when at war we have anarchy,
> There are men dead, men alive.
>
> (Last Year's Tragedy 2011b: n.pag.)

Another band in the Kenyan scene that has also come of note is Powerslide, who also address the cleavages exposed by the election violence with their song 'Banana Republic' (2019). Vocalist Willy Ojiro explained that this violence, in his view, is a vestige of Britain's divide and rule legacy. Though they had intended to address the Kenyan government as the sole focus of the song (a move they stepped away from citing 'safety' concerns), Powerslide 'instead chose to call out the system as a whole, while making reference to the post-election violence we've experienced in recent years', (Ojiro 2019: n.pag.). 'Banana Republic' calls to attention the purpose of democratic elections and the political forbearance that comes with the assumption of power:

> We seem to have all forgot, that we are one,
> All we care about now, is who sits on the throne.

You treat us all like sheep, like lambs to the slaughter,
We follow blood-red colours the streets, while you slumber in silk sheets,
Did our forefathers fight for police brutality?
No voice, no choice, but death.

(Powerslide 2019)

These songs were a necessary mechanism for coping with the traumatic events that had a great impact on their teenage years, shaping the conversations happening around them in the wake of the violence, shutting away the sense of hopelessness that the members of Last Year's Tragedy and Powerslide and anyone else who was listening may have felt. Metal, rock and punk came through at a time when a confused and upset segment of the population needed it most. 'We've created a counter-culture here that makes many people feel much more at home than they often would in their traditional and mainstream cultural environments', says Ojiro (2019: n.pag.).

Susan Shepler, whose research has focused on youth and music in Sierra Leone, a nation that was ravaged miserably by civil war, posits: 'Popular music, like other forms of popular culture, not only expresses socio-cultural reality, but generates it' (2010: 628). Shepler's research highlights one of the aspects of youth life in most African states of many feeling marginalized and a sense of hopelessness from their nation's narratives. She argues that youth critiques of the 'neo-patrimonial political system of most post-independent African states' play out in various ways (Shepler 2010: 631), notably through music as this form of expression has likely spurred the most significant form of 'democratic awakening' from youths in the post-conflict Sierra Leone (Wai cited in Shepler 2010: 633). Though the events in Kenya were not a result of life after a civil war as they were in Sierra Leone, the tragedy of seeing bodies lying in the streets, witnessing attacks on neighbours, watching your world burn in front of you were commonplace during those tumultuous weeks in Kenya. When Kenyans scream along to their favourite metal anthems, they are screaming back their lived experiences and their frustrations with the colonial vestige that lay before them.

Heavy metal was more than just a night out for metal fans in Nairobi: it meant a way of bonding, of creating a safe space for those who feel marginalized by the post-colonial capitalist trap. Metal music meant partaking in this global community, united by a form of music viewed as anathema by mainstream society at large – its own tribe split away from the status quo, surviving on its own terms (see Graham 2016: 221). Whether in Kansas, Kazakhstan, Katmandu or Kenya, metal fans are united by a common bond, one that ensures heavy metal maintains a thread of dignity, strength and honesty. Metal has an audience in Kenya precisely for this reason.

Metal has greatly assisted in the mental rebuilding needed to cope with this tragedy as many metal fans and musicians discovered a personal liberation, since 'metal is strongly connoted with freedom', (Epp 2017: 93). As Bottrell says, young people negotiate the '"constraints and opportunities for expressing who they are" by either accepting or rejecting the cultural norms, which they encounter in schools and in the community' (Bottrell cited in Rowe 2018: 53). In Kenya, many metal fans have chosen to step away from these cultural norms and focus on an identity they have embraced as their own.

Conclusion

Colonialism in Kenya was never a settled matter. It has left an ennui that has lingered for over five decades. Today's Kenyans are still living in a country that writer Billy Kahora describes as a 'half-made place' (Kahora cited in Branch 2011: 296), a country in which a crisis lies beneath all of the glass-lined edifices. While that crisis can trace its origins to colonialism, it is one with a terminus that is too far-reaching.

Kenya's heavy metal scene exists within a feeble rubric of viability less than 20 years after hitting its stride. The current scene's validation exists because musicians in Kenya have found a way to use heavy metal as a way of pushing back against the norms of their culture and country.

Among the musicians, I was fortunate enough to meet during this visit was Gun, vocalist of the hard rock band Straight Line Connection. Kenyan born and raised, Gun had only returned to Nairobi in recent years after having lived in Canada for over twenty years. Resettling into his native country with a form of music that he notes stretched well beyond the North American rehearsal spaces, Gun stated that Kenyans had found their comfort in this music because of its ability to address multitudes as well as its power to create non-cultural perspectives that values a return of 'self-worth', which he says was non-existent in previous decades (2019: n.pag.).

Participants in the Kenyan metal scene have found comfort that steps away from expected norms while fully aware that their contribution to the overall global scene is rather marginal. Yet the movement that needs to occur for a global validation is happening. Since my first visit to Kenya, the number of bands has grown and the opportunity for many of the acts to enhance their craft has improved through an increase in the availability of recording studios and opportunities to promote their music through various web pages and streaming services.

Consider, the fact that the event that united metal fans in the country, the Nairobi Metal Festival – an undertaking that many in the local scene would have dismissed in previous years as just a fantasy – has since become an annual event.[52] The festival has become an outlet for local musicians to interact with the business acumen and musical acuity of international bands who are able to share professional insight into performing and recording at a level that Kenyans would have likely never accessed previously. Aphasia's Daniel Mwangi notes the visits from international musicians are helping the Kenyan scene in big ways. 'We learn a few things from them. They bring quality to the table' (Banchs 2019: n.pag.).

Several generations removed from the British exit in East Africa, Kenya's identity has been shaped by misguided trajectories as the initial wounds left by the colonial empire have not healed, nor have they even come close to being stitched. However, there have been sparks of brilliance that have shaped the nation, including a redrafted constitution that guarantees Kenyans a protection of the civil rights necessary to promulgate a healthy democracy. Since the first multi-party elections in 2002, the nation has slowly transitioned into one that has presented more opportunities for its citizens. Yet it is a nation with too many vestiges of its past still within reach. Economic disparity is still incredibly visible. Corruption remains ubiquitous. Authoritarian streaks continue (though they are held in check by the constitution). Police forces are still fighting to gain the trust of a society that gave up on them decades ago. And atavistic proclivities still curse the nation. However, Kenyans live with hope.

It is within this hope that the Kenyan metal scene finds itself crafting its own narrative of what is possible in their bruised nation, and what is possible for themselves.

Conclusion

Confronting Realities through Heavy Metal

2020 was a distressing year.

With seven billion routines disrupted simultaneously amid the COVID-19 pandemic, life seemed bleak for those who had never encountered such challenges. In a continent where less than half of its 54 countries have access to modern health care facilities (Nkengasong cited in Anna 2020), many worried that Africa would not fare well, especially as countries in the Global North, with widely advanced healthcare systems, began to see spikes in cases and deaths.

The world was wrong. Just as the United States (my country) began to surpass 260,000 deaths, the entire African continent – home to over one billion people – was estimated to have only a fraction of that, with just over 33,000 reported deaths at the end of November (World Health Organization 2020). Though both numbers, as well as the unfortunate surpassing of over a million deaths worldwide is heartbreaking, Africa was the one continent that knew how to handle such an event. Africa has been here before. Notably, the recent Ebola outbreak in 2014, and the HIV/AIDS crisis taught Africa how to respond to such a crisis, how to mobilize supplies and how to spread correct information that instructed the public on the necessary precautions to curtail the spread of this virus. Yet the world seemingly took nothing from the lessons African fortitude provided (Attiah 2020). This is the story of Africa.

But Africa, once again, was proving the world wrong.

COVID-19, however, exposed global income disparities to a level previously unseen, and will likely set over a hundred million people on a course towards extreme poverty (World Bank 2020), including citizens in Kenya, Ghana, Togo and South Africa. Healthcare systems, too, were also pushed beyond their limits in even the most developed nations.

For Dark Suburb in Accra, this only highlighted why their band needs to continue calling attention to the plight of those inhabiting slums. Ghana, like other nations in West Africa, reported cases and deaths much lower than expected, but the reality for many in the nation was that their economic situations would likely be altered.

For the metal scenes, 2020 stood to hamper their progress. Yet, a global lockdown proved to be a positive opportunity for acts to showcase their sound with metal fans around the world who would be glued to computer monitors instead of stages.

Crystal Axis finally made their European debut – virtually. Duma, a Kenyan electronic-metal duo, garnered global attention with the release of their debut (O'Boyle 2020; Kalia 2020), once again showing the world that the unexpected is what is best expected from Africa. Others such as Arka'n Asrafokor performed to a global audience via a recorded performance for AfroPunk (Planet Afropunk 2020), and the annual South African metal festival, Metal4Africa SummerFest, went virtual (Metal4Africa 2020), while many bands, including several highlighted in this book, used this opportunity to focus on creating new music.

Africans have already survived colonialism, civil conflicts that ravaged their nations, leadership failures, life in failed states, and numerous other epidemics and waves of unprecedented famines. Yet Africans carried on. Amidst a pandemic, Africans would never waver. This was just another bump in an obstacle-riddled road in a continent accustomed to its share of challenges.

The metal world understands this, too. If the world has continually cast their doubts on Africa, they are aware of the arduous task of convincing metal fans that their art and their voices should be taken seriously. Heavy metal exists for this reason: to amplify the voices of the marginalized, the destitute and those ready to pursue the change that they see fit. Heavy metal is the voice for many Africans because it is what is needed to validate their existence and to show the world that they are here, and ready to be heard.

This book has cast a light on the marginalization of African art and voices, and the assumptions cast down on the idea that Africans could never do what Westerners are doing, that they could never think the way Westerners are thinking and that they could never respond to tragedy in a manner that would behove a large population with scarcer resources than most on the planet.

If the COVID-19 pandemic revealed something else, apart from the health and economic disparities that exist in marginalized corners, it is that African contributions will likely continue to be pushed aside in favour of something a bit more familiar to Westerners.

And while they are attuned as to how they are viewed, African musicians are still very aware of the challenges that lay ahead in proving Westerners that they, too, belong on the same stages. And, they are quite content in doing so their way: sharing their lived experiences, their struggles and their ways through their music. What remains to be seen, however, is how serious African creativity will be taken in the coming years.

African metal bands are ready to show the rest of the world, yet again, they are wrong about Africa!

Endnotes

1. Meaning 'warrior' in Ewe.
2. British Togoland would eventually be incorporated into their Gold Coast colony in 1956, which would gain independence the following year and be renamed as Ghana.
3. Eyadéma was Africa's longest serving head of state at the time of his death.
4. Sepultura's music, for example, tends to be referred to often as a 'tribal' metal act (Wieder-horn 2017: n.pag.).
5. Within ten minutes of my arrival into Togo, the vehicle I was travelling in was stopped by police officers while my driver and Rock instructed me to just keep quiet as they would handle the affair. Two officers asked the driver to get out of the vehicle and open the trunk. Through the space between the opening of the trunk and the rear window, I noted the driver passing a few banknotes into the officer's hand. Embarrassed by the incident, Rock explained that bribery in Togo is also fairly common.
6. For privacy reasons, I am omitting the name of the producer.
7. An initiative set by the member states of the United Nations in September 2000 with the aim of – by 2015 – ending extreme poverty and hunger; achieving global primary education; empowering women and promoting gender equality; reducing child mortality; promoting maternal health; fighting malaria, HIV/AIDS and other diseases; to promote environmental sustainability; and to develop a universal partnership for development.
8. Exactly how many NGOs, whether local, or international, are operating in Ghana is difficult to determine. One 2018 estimation has at least 200 (Suburu 2018).
9. Of note: Kru, an ethnic group from Liberia noted for their seafaring acumen, took to the guitar after learning the instrument from Western sailors. Kru sailors would often entertain themselves by playing the guitar during their stops, passing on Calypso music and European music (mainly Portuguese) to other West Africans, including Ghanaians. Jacob Sam, who was the first highlife recording artist in 1928, recording on the Zonophone label, was taught how to play the guitar by a Kru sailor (Collins 1996: xii).
10. The practice of enforcing censorship from the colonial government continued through independence as even theater productions were put on alert if they took pro-independence stances (Collins 2006: 175).

11. It has been suggested, however, that racial discrimination policies similar to those of neighbouring South Africa and Zimbabwe also existed in colonial era Botswana (see Mgadla 2014).

12. The term Batswana is the demonym for more than one person from Botswana, while Motswana defines the singular.

13. A portmanteau of the words 'Motswana', the pluralized demonym of 'Batswana', or a person from Botswana, and 'rockers'. The term 'MaRock' has been embraced locally by the participants of the scene and widely used to speak specifically of the fans by the photographers.

14. Formal interview requests had been made to all of the photographers cited in this chapter. If the photographers were not interviewed directly, I drew from interviews that were published elsewhere. All quotes are cited accordingly. I must also note that during my first trip to Botswana in 2012, I had a chance meeting with Daniele Tamagni while he was photographing this scene. Sadly, Tamagni passed away in 2017 at the age of 42.

15. Marshall is also the only one of the photographers that is an active participant of an African metal scene.

16. The 1985 film, directed by George Miller and George Ogilvie was released as *Mad Max Beyond Thunderdome*.

17. Brincat has a career in theater as both an actor and director. While living in Botswana he worked as a drama teacher and also directed productions.

18. Sbrana, along with his father Ivo (Nosey Road) are featured in Marshall's *Visions of Renegades* set.

19. Aside from major outlets, interests from commercial bloggers has also proved relevant as a quick YouTube search yields professionally recorded videos from sites such as the Great Big Story (2018), and the Dutch television series *Metropolis* (2013; see also Okoli 2017; Lelliot 2015).

20. This term, like Cape Malay and Black, are used non-pejoratively in the country. Though a Westerner may view the usage of these terms as condescending, I have chosen to use Coloured and Black in this text as I would in South Africa.

21. Former president Hendrik Verwoerd once compared television to 'atomic bomb and poison gas', while the former minister for Posts and Telegraphs, Dr. Albert Hertzog, said that televisions could lead to the dissemination of communism, immortally and race mixing (Roux 2017: n.pag.)

22. South African Bureau of Standards.

23. This claim, also made by Lulat (2008: 426) fell on deaf ears to the South Africans I personally interviewed, who all noted that they were well aware of who these musicians were and had explained that they were familiar with their music, which they possibly discovered once apartheid ended. However, I must note that, while I am not choosing to ignore my primary sources, all of the indications here from scholars and researchers indicate that Black artists were not sold in South Africa.

24. Sharpeville is a township in the Gauteng province, south of Johannesburg.
25. A detailed list of bands that existed during the era is not possible, as there were many active metal bands during the early 80s as well as hard rock bands to which some fans can point as being heavy metal, a descriptive term that was, and is still, fairly subjective. For an extensive list of rock bands from the 1960s on, The South African Rock Encyclopedia (2020) provides a great resource.
26. Non-Whites could serve as volunteers.
27. All of the musicians assumed monikers that were intended to be humorous. Koos Kombuis, the moniker of celebrated musician André le Roux du Toit, translates to 'Chamber pot Kitchen'. Johannes Kerkorrel, the moniker of Ralph John Rabie, is the name of a Dutch organ. Bernoldus Niemand was the moniker of James Phillips.
28. Military service was mandatory for all able-bodied White males during apartheid.
29. Title translated from Afrikaans: *Rock Musiek: Die reg om te weet*.
30. It should be noted that various police departments in the United States also had 'Satan hunters' following the moral panics that precipitated in the mid-to-late 1980s. Some of their material for law enforcement agencies included items such as ritualistic crime scene manuals, slides of ritualistic crime scenes and even 'calendars of supposed Satanic celebration days. These items were widely used by 'experts' on Satanic cult crime at police training seminars and at community meetings. Notable 'experts' in the United States included Robert 'Jerry' Simandl, Pamala Klein and Pat Pulling' (Victor 1993: 245–35).
31. It has been speculated that the Occult Unit has since reformed into different units within the police force (Bevan 2006).
32. I have chosen to omit the victim's name. Three other school employees suffered serious wounds in the attack (Pindral 2018).
33. The band performed under the moniker $X \, \Xi \, \Sigma$, which translates to '666'.
34. The band is the subject of a documentary, *Fokofpolisiekar: Forgive Them for They Know Not What They Do* (Little 2009), that chronicles their origins and their impact on the South African music scene.
35. As of 2014, it is estimated that 340,000 South Africans who emigrated have since moved back (Flanagan 2014).
36. Some would return within a few years as the artists who left did so because they were now free to travel to the regions of the world they were previously unable to access due to the political sanctions on the country. Artists could now meet others who also shared the same ambitions while introducing themselves to new ideas and gaining the business acumen necessary to make South African art and music more global.
37. Robertson does not make specific designations for Coloureds, or other non-White South Africans, in her paper.
38. At the request of TK's family, his name and country of origin have been concealed for privacy.

39. It is estimated that over 98,000 Kenyan men served the British during the East Africa campaign (Killingray 2010: 44) against Italian East Africa (an area that today encompasses Ethiopia, Eritrea, Djibouti and Somalia), Japanese encroachment in Madagascar and the Burma campaign.

40. The song's origins and songwriter are often disputed as it has also been claimed that 'Malaika' was written in 1945 by Tanzanian Adam Salim. William's claim to the song came by virtue of recording it with his band The Jambo Boys in 1960. As is noted throughout travelling in East Africa and interviewing and meeting journalist and musicians, when it comes to identifying who the song's proper writer is, it depends who you ask! For the sake of clarity here, I am identifying William's version as it was the recording from Worrod's studio that became a hit.

41. I noticed throughout my travels that musicians rarely claimed ownership over the instruments on which they performed, notably drummers, who could only practice drums during band practices. This is why musicians in African nations who often joined more than one band were highly cherished – they were better rehearsed.

42. Internet use in Kenya has become fairly widespread since its arrival in the country in the mid 90s. It is estimated that 98 per cent of the national population has a mobile phone, which in turn enables Kenyans to use the internet, as the phone is the primary means of connection for 96 per cent of all internet users (Kemp 2020).

43. Kenya was not a country in which they conducted research.

44. Portions of this interview were published in Germany's *Legacy Magazine* (Irtenkauf 2017). My interview was worked into a narrative that was published in German, however, I conducted the interview in English via email on behalf of the magazine.

45. The song is performed in Kenya's colonial language, English, for the purpose of establishing the band's presence in Western markets. I have written about the use of language in the Kenyan rock and metal scene elsewhere (see Banchs 2016b).

46. Former Presidential candidate Francois Fillon.

47. Aroni has since left the band.

48. *Baba* is the Swahili word for 'father' or 'dad'.

49. The language, one 'that emerged from the complex multilingual situation of Nairobi City' (Githiora 2002: 159) is of note here because, much like the heavy metal scene in the country, Sheng has also emerged from this millennial generation.

50. The largest ethnic group in Kenya, a 2019 estimate shows that around 17 per cent of the population is Kikuyu (CIA 2020).

51. An inquiry commissioned by the Kenyan government in 2008, known as the Waki Commission, found this to be the case and the matter was handed over to the International Criminal Courts (ICC), who named six primary suspects as instigators in this violence (Verini 2016). Among those named was Uhuru Kenyatta, who, at the time of writing, is the president of Kenya.

52. As was the case with live music events globally, the 2020 version of the Nairobi Metal Festival was canceled due to concerns surrounding COVID-19.

References

Acemoglu, Daron, Johnson, Simon and Robinson, James A. (2001), 'An African success story: Botswana', *SSRN*, July, pp. 1–37, http://dx.doi.org/10.2139/ssrn.290791. Accessed 13 July 2021.

Adepitan, Ade (2016), 'Where traditional African culture and heavy metal collide', BBC Travel, 5 February, https://www.bbc.com/travel/article/20151218-where-traditional-african-culture-and-heavy-metal-collide. Accessed 10 June 2019.

Ajulu, Rok (2002), 'Politicized ethnicity, competitive politics and conflict in Kenya: A historical perspective', *African Studies*, 61:2, pp. 251–68.

Akyeampong, Oheneba Akwasi and Yankholmes, Aaron (2016), 'Profiling masquerade festival attendees in Ghana', *Event Management*, 20, pp. 285–96.

Allen, Lara (2019), 'Kwela', in D. Horn, J. Shepard (eds), *Bloomsbury Encyclopedia of Popular Music of the World Vol. XII, Genres: Sub-Saharan Africa*, New York: Bloomsbury Academic, pp. 358–62.

Anna, Cara (2020), 'As US struggles, Africa's COVID-19 response is praised', *Associated Press*, 22 September, https://apnews.com/article/virus-outbreak-ghana-africa-pandemics-donaldtrump-0a31db50d816a463a6a29bf86463aaa9. Accessed 20 November 2020.

Appert, Catherine M. (2011), 'Rappin griots: Producing the local in Senegalese hip-hop', in P. Khalil Saucier (ed.), *Native Tongues: An African Hip-Hop Reader*, New Jersey: Africa World Press, pp. 3–22.

Appert, Catherine M. (2016), 'Locating hip-hop origins: Popular music and tradition in senegal', *Africa*, 86:2, pp. 237–62.

Arka'n Asrafokor (2019), *Zã Keli*, digital, Togo: Self-released.

Aroni, Djae (2017), e-mail to author, 14 October.

Astill, James (2002), 'Violence mars final days of Kenya's election campaign', *The Guardian*, 26 December, https://www.theguardian.com/world/2002/dec/27/kenya.jamesastill. Accessed 2 April 2019.

Attiah, Karen (2020), 'Africa has defied the covid-19 nightmare scenarios: We shouldn't be surprised', *The Washington Post*, 22 September, https://www.washingtonpost.com/opinions/2020/09/22/africa-has-defied-covid-19-nightmare-scenarios-we-shouldnt-be-surprised/. Accessed 20 November 2020.

Avelar, Idelber (2003), 'Heavy metal music in postdictatorial Brazil: Sepultura and the coding of nationality in sound', *Journal of Latin American Cultural Studies*, 12:3, pp. 329–46.

Avelar, Idelber (2011), 'Otherwise national: Locality and power in the art of Sepultura', in J. Wallach, H. M. Berger and P. Greene (eds), *Metal Rules the Globe: Heavy Metal Music Around the World*, Durham: Duke University Press, pp. 135–58.

Awumbila, Mariama, Owusu, George and Kofi Teye, Joseph (2014), 'Can urban migration into slums reduce poverty?: Evidence from Ghana', *Migrating out of Poverty: Research Program Consortium*, Working Paper 13, Brighton: University of Sussex, http://www.migratingout-ofpoverty.org/files/file.php?name=wp-13---awumbila-owusu-teye-2014-can-rural-urban-migration-into-slums-reduce-poverty-final.pdf&site=354. Accessed 27 August 2020.

Babenco, Héctor (1991), *At Play in the Field of the Lord*, USA: Universal Pictures.

Banchs, Edward (2013), 'Desert sounds—Kalahari metalheads pursue a dream', *The Guardian*, 10 February, https://www.theguardian.com/world/2013/feb/10/kalahari-metalheads. Accessed 30 July, 2021.

Banchs, Edward (2016a), *Heavy Metal Africa: Life, Passion and Heavy Metal in the Forgotten Continent*, Tarentum: Word Association Publisher.

Banchs, Edward (2016b), 'Swahili-tounged devils: Kenya's heavy metal at the crossroads of identity', *Metal Music Studies*, 2:3, pp. 311–24.

Banchs, Edward (2019), 'Nairobi Metal Festival: Inside Kenya's flourishing metal scene', *Metal Hammer*, 30 October, https://www.loudersound.com/features/nairobi-metal-festival-in-side-kenyas-flourishing-metal-scene. Accessed 30 October 2019.

Barnett, Eroll (2012a), 'Meeting up with Botswana's "metal heads"', *CNN: Inside Africa*, 2 July, https://edition.cnn.com/videos/international/2012/07/02/inside-africa-botswana-met-al-music-a.cnn. Accessed 29 May 2019.

Barnett, Eroll (2012b), 'The sound of Botswana's metal music', *CNN: Inside Africa*, 2 July, https://www.cnn.com/videos/international/2012/07/02/inside-africa-botswana-metal-music-c.cnn. Accessed 29 May 2019.

Barnett, Eroll (2015), 'Rebels with a cause: Botswana's heavy metal heads', *CNN: African Voices*, 8 December, https://edition.cnn.com/2012/06/29/world/africa/botswana-heavy-met-al-heads/index.html. Accessed 29 May 2019.

Bates, Robert H. (1981), *Markets and States in Tropical Africa*, Berkeley: University of California Press.

Bayton, Mavis (1997), 'Women and the electric guitar', in S. Whiteley (ed.), *Sexing the Groove: Popular Music and Gender*, London: Routledge, pp. 37–49.

BBC (2013), 'In pictures: Renegades—the heavy metal sub-culture of Botswana', 20 February, https://www.bbc.com/news/in-pictures-21509571. Accessed 10 June 2019.

Beaumont, Peter (2019), 'Rotten eggs: E-waste from Europe poisons Ghana's food chain', *The Guardian*, 24 April, https://www.theguardian.com/global-development/2019/apr/24/rotten-chicken-eggs-e-waste-from-europe-poisons-ghana-food-chain-agbogbloshie-accra. Accessed 25 August 2020.

Bell, Chris (2013), 'Apartheid's roots: The native's land acts', BBC History, 19 June, http://wwwnews.live.bbc.co.uk/history/0/22786616. Accessed 8 November 2018.

Belcher, Stephen, (2004), 'Studying griots: Recent work in mande studies', *African Studies Review*, 47:3, pp. 172–86.

Beltran, Louis Ramiro (1978), 'Communication and cultural domination: U.S.-Latin America case', *Media Asia*, 5, pp. 183–92.

Bevan, Stephen (2006), 'South African police accused of ignoring ritual murders', *The Telegraph*, 26 March, https://www.telegraph.co.uk/news/worldnews/africaandindianocean/1514025/South-African-police-accused-of-ignoring-ritual-murders.html. Accessed 10 June 2020.

Bhabha, Homi K. (1984), 'Of mimicry and man: The ambivalence of colonial discourse', *Discipleship: A Special Issue on Psychoanalysis*, 28, pp. 125–33.

Bhabha, Homi K. (1990), 'The third space: Interview with Homi Bhabha', in J. Rutherford (ed.), *Identity Community, Culture, Difference*, London: Lawrence & Wishart, pp. 207–21.

Bond, Catherine (2002) '"Kenyans" joy as Kibaki is sworn in', *CNN*, 30 December, http://www.cnn.com/2002/WORLD/africa/12/30/kenya.acclaim/. Accessed 2 April 2019.

Branch, Daniel (2011), *Kenya: Between Hope and Despair, 1963–2011*, New Haven: Yale University Press.

Brincat, Aldo (2018), 'Foreign Nationals', Aldo Brincat Official Website, http://www.brincatproductions.co.za/?fbclid=IwAR09CYmdFw2oQ7hamGjvvgE0kB2Omr-ZCz1S9cgm9K2AsGPOUHC7W2JT18w#prettyPhoto%5Biframes%5D/44/. Accessed 31 May 2019 [no longer available; access to photograph only: http://www.aldobrincat.com/collections.html. Accessed 4 October 2021].

Brincat, Aldo (2019), e-mail to author, 28 October.

Brooks, Richard (1955), *The Blackboard Jungle*, USA: Metro-Goldwyn-Mayer.

Butler, Judith (1990), *Gender Trouble: Feminism and the Subversion of Identity*, New York and London: Routledge.

Byrnes, Rita M. (ed.) (1996), 'South Africa: A country study', U.S. Library of Congress, http://countrystudies.us/south-africa/44.htm. Accessed 12 December 2018.

Caravanos, Jack, Clark, Edith, Fuller, Richard and Lambertson, Calah (2011), 'Assessing worker and environmental chemical exposure risks at an e-waste and disposal site in Accra, Ghana' *Journal of Health Pollution*, 1:1, pp. 16–25.

Cardwell, Tom (2017), 'Battle jackets, authenticity and "material individuality"', *Metal Music Studies*, 3:3, pp. 437–58.

Ceasar, Ed (2020), 'The rock', *The New Yorker*, 3 February, pp. 32–45.

Chama, M. A., Amankwa, Ebenezer Forkuo and Oteng-Ababio, Martin (2014), 'Trace metal levels of the odaw river sediments at the agbogbloshie e-waste recycling site', *Journal of Science and Technology*, 34:1, pp. 1–8.

Channel 24 (2012), 'Anti-Gaga protest flair up in Cape Town', 16 November, https://www.channel24.co.za/Music/News/Anti-Gaga-protests-flare-up-in-Cape-Town-20121116. Accessed 9 August 2019.

Channel 24 (2017), 'We chat to US metal act DevilDriver ahead of their SA tour', 11 April, https://www.channel24.co.za/Music/News/we-chat-to-us-metal-act-devildriver-ahead-of-their-sa-tour-20170410. Accessed 9 August 2019.

Chapman, Tracy (1989), *Crossroads*, CD: Elektra Records.

Chasant, Muntaka (2019), 'A young man burning electrical wires to recover copper at Agbog-bloshie, September 2019', Wikimedia, https://en.wikipedia.org/wiki/Agbogbloshie#/media/File:Agbogbloshie,Ghana-September2019.jpg. Accessed 11 November 2020.

Chikha, Chokiri Ben and Arnaut, Karel (2013), 'Staging/caging "otherness" in the postcolony: Spectres of the human zoo', *Critical Arts*, 27:6, pp. 661–83.

Christie, Sean (2013), 'Ten years of crazy fokken rock', *Mail & Guardian*, 13 September, https://mg.co.za/article/2013-09-13-ten-years-of-crazy-fokken-rock. Accessed 28 June 2019.

Chukura, Ngozi and Rolinec, Petra (2017), 'Meet Botswana's fearsomely vibrant heavy metal subculture, the marock', *Afropunk*, 24 April, https://afropunk.com/2017/04/meet-bot-swanas-fearsomely-vibrant-heavy-metal-subculture-the-marock/. Accessed 31 May 2019.

CIA (2017), 'The world factbook: Togo', https://www.cia.gov/the-world-factbook/countries/togo/, 1 July, Accessed 25 November 2019.

CIA (2020), 'The world factbook: Kenya', https://www.cia.gov/the-world-factbook/countries/kenya/, Accessed 27 October 2020.

Ciolfi, Tecla (2019), 'Ghanzi: A metal community in arms', *Jägermeister After Dark*, 12 June, https://jagermeisterafterdark.co.za/ghanzi-a-metal-community-in-arms/. Accessed 19 June 2019.

Cockar, Talal (2019), e-mail to author, 25 April.

Cockar, Talal (2020), e-mail to author, 27 October.

Cohen, Sara (1997), 'Men making a scene: Rock music and the production of gender', in S. Whiteley (ed.), *Sexing the Groove: Popular Music and Gender*, New York and London: Routledge, pp. 17–36.

Cohen, Sara (1999), 'Scenes', in B. Horner and T. Swiss (eds), *Key Terms in Popular Music and Culture*, Massachusetts: Blackwell Publishers, pp. 239–50.

Cole, Teju (2012), 'The white savior industrial complex', *The Atlantic*, 21 March, https://www.theatlantic.com/international/archive/2012/03/the-white-savior-industrial-complex/254843/. Accessed 19 July 2019.

Collins, John (1989), 'The early history of West African highlife music', *Popular Music*, 8:3, pp. 221–30.

Collins, John (1996), *Highlife Time*, 2nd ed., Ghana: Anansesem Publications Ltd.

Collins, John (2006), 'One hundred years of censorship in Ghanaian popular music perfor-mance', in M. Drewett and M. Cloonan (eds), *Popular Music Censorship in Africa*, London, UK: Ashgate, pp. 171–86.

Collins, John (2009), 'Popular dance music and the media', in K. Njogu and J. Middleton (eds), *Media and Identity in Africa*, Edinburgh: Edinburgh University Press Ltd and International African Institute, pp. 162–70.

Collins, John (2019), 'Afro-rock', in D. Horn and J. Shepherd (eds), *Bloomsbury Encyclopedia of Popular Music of the World Vol. XII, Genres: Sub-Saharan Africa*, pp. 30–34.

Connelly, Christoper (1982), 'Apartheid rock: Despite a United Nations boycott, American musicians from Frank Sinatra to Tina Turner still play South Africa', *Rolling Stone*, 10 June, https://www.rollingstone.com/music/music-news/apartheid-rock-108260/. Accessed 22 January 2018.

Coplan, David (1982), 'The urbanisation of African music', *Popular Music*, 2, pp. 112–29.

Coupland, Reginald (1939), *The Exploitation of East Africa, 1856–90: The Slave Trade and the Scramble*, London: Faber and Faber.

Cowling, Natalie (2018), e-mail to author, 8 January.

Crook, Richard C. (1999), '"No Party" politics and local democracy in Africa: Rawlings Ghana in the 1990s and the "Ugandan Model"', *Democratization*, 6:4, pp. 114–38.

Cruise O'Brien, Donal (1996), 'A lost generation: Youth identity and state decay in West Africa', in R. Werbner and T. Ranger (eds), *Post-Colonial Identities in Africa*, London: Zed Books, pp. 55–74.

Crystal Axis (2018), 'Leopold', *Leopold*, digital single, Kenya: Self-released.

Crystal Axis (2019), 'Nyayo House', *Nyayo House*, digital single, Kenya: Self-released.

Dark, Suburb (2014), 'Get Out', *Get Out*, digital single, Ghana: Self-released.

Dark, Suburb (2015), 'I Dey Feel You Die', *I Dey Feel You Die*, digital single, Ghana: Self-released.

Dark, Suburb (2017a), 'Colorblind', *The Start Looks Like the End*, digital LP, Ghana: Dark Suburb Music.

Dark, Suburb (2017b), 'Demons', *The Start Looks Like the End*, digital LP, Ghana: Dark Suburb Music.

Dark, Suburb (2017c), 'Lunatic Question', *The Start Looks the End*, digital LP, Ghana: Dark Suburb Music.

Dark, Suburb (2017d), *The Start Looks Like the End*, digital LP, Ghana: Dark Suburb Music.

Dark, Suburb (2020a), Facebook post, 16 August, https://www.facebook.com/darksuburbmusic/posts/827788071087154. Accessed 17 August 2020 [no longer available].

Dark, Suburb (2020b), '@chalewoteofficial vibes.virtual concert fit pap!!!', Facebook, 26 August, https://www.facebook.com/watch/?v=2406903739602373&extid=KosFyQTmnjS4v6LT. Accessed 15 July 2021.

Dark, Suburb (n.d.), Facebook page, https://www.facebook.com/darksuburbmusic. Accessed 17 October 2020.

Desmond, Matthew (2016) *Evicted: Poverty and Profit in the American City*, Broadway Books: New York.

Doan, Petra and Oduro, Charles Yaw (2011), 'Patterns of population growth in Peri-Urban Accra, Ghana', *International Journal of Urban and Regional Research*, 36:6, pp. 1–20.

Dolan, Julia (1987), 'Four teens make suicide pact, die of carbon monoxide poisoning', *Associated Press*, 12 March, https://apnews.com/article/36e3d4ac9c496ab414af8793e089ca4d. Accessed 4 November 2020.

Donnelly, Denise A., Cook, Kimberly J., Ausdale, Debra Van and Foley, Lara (2005), 'White privilege, color blindness and services to battered women', *Violence Against Women*, 11:1, pp. 6–37.

Don't Party (2016), 'Satanic panic: Behind South Africa's fear of the occult', *Medium*, 22 February, https://medium.com/@DontParty/satanic-panic-behind-south-africa-s-fear-of-the-occult-6d8d09ea3393. Accessed 22 January 2018.

Dowden, Richard (2009), *Africa: Altered States, Ordinary Miracles*, New York: Public Affairs.

Drewett, Michael (2003), 'Music in the struggle to end apartheid: South Africa', in M. Cloonan and R. Garafolo (eds), *Policing Pop*, Philadelphia: Temple University Press, pp. 153–65.

Economist (2008), 'Between staying and going: Violent crime and political turmoil are adding to South Africa's brain drain', *The Economist: Briefing*, 25 September, https://www.economist.com/briefing/2008/09/25/between-staying-and-going. Accessed 8 June 2018.

Emielu, Austin (2011), 'Some theoretical perspectives on African popular music', *Popular Music*, 30:3, pp. 371–88.

Enrico (2019), in-person interview with E. Banchs, Lomé, Togo, 22 September.

Epp, Andre (2017), 'Diversity in metal politics', in M. Elovaara and B. Bardine (eds), *Connective Metal to Culture: Unity in Disparity*, Bristol: Intellect Press, pp. 81–98.

Epstein, Debbie (1998), 'Marked men: Whiteness and masculinity', *Agenda: Empowering Women for Gender Equity*, 37, pp. 49–59.

Erasmus, Paul (2004), 'Roger, me and the scorpion: Working for the South African security services during apartheid', in M. Korpe (ed.), *Shoot the Singer! Music Censorship Today*, London: Zed Books, pp 73–81.

Ewens, Graham (2000), 'Fundi Konde: A legend of East African music', *The Guardian*, 20 July, https://www.theguardian.com/news/2000/jul/21/guardianobituaries. Accessed 26 April 2019.

Falkof, Nicky (2012), '"Satan has come to Rietfontein": Race in South Africa's satanic panic', *Journal of Southern African Studies*, 38:4, https://www.researchgate.net/publication/262961669_%27Satan_has_come_to_Rietfontein%27_Race_in_South_Africa%27s_Satanic_Panic. pp. 1–21.

Fanon, Frantz (2008), *Black Skin, White Masks* (trans. R. Philcox), New York: Grove Press.

Feldt, Torsten, Fobil, Julius N., Wittsiepe, Jürgen, Wilhelm, Michael, Till, Holger, Zoufaly, Alexander, Burchard, Gerd and Göen, Thomas (2013), 'High levels of PAH-metabolites in urine of e-waste recycling workers from Agbogbloshie, Ghana', *Science of the Total Environment*, 466–67, pp. 369–76.

Ferguson, Robyn (2020), correspondence via email, 14 September.

Flanagan, Jane (2014), 'Why white South Africans are coming home', *BBC News*, 3 May, https://www.bbc.com/news/world-africa-27252307. Accessed 20 June 2020.

Fleetwood, Mick (1981), *Mick Fleetwood: The Visitor*, LP, UK: RCA Records.

Fleetwood, Mick and Shapiro, Micky (1981), *Mick Fleetwood: The Visitor*, USA: n.p.

Fokofpolisiekar (2003), *As Jy Met Vuur Speel Sal Jy Brand*, CD: Rhythm Records.

Foster, Hal (1995), 'The artist as ethnographer?', in G. E. Marcus and F. R. Myers (eds), *The Traffic in Culture: Refiguring Art and Anthropology*, Berkeley: University of California Press, pp. 302–09.

Gagakuma, Seterwo (1998), 'Ghana: The 2020 vision', *African Business*, 238 (December), https://www.questia.com/magazine/1G1-53436219/ghana-the-2020-vision. Accessed 8 September 2020 [no longer available].

Gaisie, Eric, Kim, Hyung Min and Han, Sun Sheng (2019), 'Accra towards a city-region: Devolution, spatial development and urban challenges', *Cities: The International Journal of Urban Policy and Planning*, 95 (December), pp. 1–11.

Gallagher, Charles (2003), 'Color-blind privilege: The social and political functions of erasing the color line in post race America', *Race, Gender & Class*, 10:4, pp. 22–37.

Gidi Gidi Maji Maji (2002) *Unbwogable*, CD, Kenya: A'mish Records.

Githiora, Chege (2002), 'Sheng: Peer language, Swahili dialect or emerging Creole?', *Journal of African Cultural Studies*, 15:2, pp. 159–81.

Gligorijevic, Jelena (2011), 'The global and the local in Max Cavalera's music projects', *Etnomusikologian vuosikirja*, 23, pp. 140–64.

Goode, Erich and Ben-Yehuda, Nachman (1994), 'Moral panics: Culture, politics, and social construction', *Annual Review of Sociology*, 20, pp.149–170.

Graham, Stephen (2016), *Sounds of the Underground: A Cultural, Political and Aesthetic Mapping of Underground and Fringe Music*, Ann Arbor: University of Michigan Press.

Great Big Story (2018), 'The death metal bangers of Botswana', 6 July, https://www.youtube.com/watch?v=BVYz9o4n-mA. Accessed 6 June 2020.

Greene, Paul D. (2011), 'Electronic and affective overdrive: Tropes of transgression in Nepal's heavy metal scene', in J. Wallach, H. M. Berger and P. D. Greene (eds), *Metal Rules the Globe: Heavy Metal Music Around the Globe*, Durham: Duke University Press, pp. 109–34.

Grobler, Fienie (2008), 'Krugersdorp school rocked by "Satanic" killing', *Mail & Guardian*, 18 August, https://mg.co.za/article/2008-08-18-krugersdorp-school-rocked-by-satanic-killing. Accessed 15 August 2019.

Grundlingh, Albert (2004), '"Rocking the boat" in South Africa? *Voëlvry* music and Afrikaans anti-apartheid social protest in the 1980s', *International Journal of African Historical Studies*, 37:3, pp. 483–514.

Gun (2019), e-mail to author, 17 November.

Hale, Thomas (1997), 'From the griot of *Roots* to the roots of *Griot*: A new look at the origins of a controversial African term for bard', *Oral Tradition* 12:2, pp. 249–78.

Hamm, Charles (1985), 'Rock 'n' roll in a very strange society', *Popular Music*, 5, pp. 159–74.

Hamm, Charles (1988) *Afro-American Music, South Africa, and Apartheid*, I.S.A.M Monographs 28, New York: Institute for Studies in American Music.

Harneit-Sievers, Axel and Peters, Ralph-Michael (2008), 'Kenya's 2007 general election and its aftershocks', *African Spectrum: Horn of Africa*, 43:1, pp. 133–44.

Hendricks, C. C. (2017), 'Bang your head to the "Beat" of non-conformity', in M. Elovaara and B. Bardine (eds), *Connecting Metal to Culture: Unity in Disparity*, pp. 119–42, Bristol: Intellect.

Herman, Audrey (2019), 'Togo: Les métalleux font du bruit', *TV5 Monde Togo*, 29 September, https://information.tv5monde.com/video/togo-les-metalleux-font-du-bruit. Accessed 29 September 2019.

Hill, Rosemary Lucy (2015), 'Using women's listening pleasure to challenge the notion of hard rock and metal as "Masculine Music"', in T. M. Karjalainen and K. Kärki (eds), *Modern Heavy Metal: Markets, Practices and Cultures, International Academic Research Conference, Helsinki, Finland, 8–12 June*, Finland: Aalto University Publication Series, pp. 240–46.

Hoad, Catherine (2014), '*Ons is saam*—Afrikaans metal and rebuilding whiteness in the rainbow nation', *International Journal of Community Music*, 7:2, pp. 189–204.

Hochschild, Adam (1998), *King Leopold's Ghost: A Story of Greed, Terror and Heroism in Colonial Africa*, Boston: Mariner Books.

Iliffe, John (2005), *Honour in African History*, Cambridge: Cambridge University Press.

Index Mundi (2019), 'Ghana—Population living in slums (% of urban population)', https://www.indexmundi.com/facts/ghana/indicator/EN.POP.SLUM.UR.ZS. Accessed 25 September 2020.

IOL News (2008), 'Devildriver concert moved to Alberton', *IOL News*, 23 October, https://www.iol.co.za/news/south-africa/devildriver-concert-moved-to-alberton-421598. Accessed 9 August 2019.

Iron Maiden (1981), *Killers*, LP, UK: EMI.

Irony Destroyed (2019), 'Najiskia Kuua Tena', *Najiskia Kuua Tena,* digital single, Kenya: Self-released.

Irtenkauf, Dominik (2017), 'Africa metal double feature: Roar of Heroes & Crystal Axis', *Legacy Magazine*, 111 (November/December), p. 22.

Israel, Dave (2020), e-mail to author, 8 June.

James, Lawrence (2017), *Empires in the Sun: The Struggle for the Mastery of Africa*, New York: Pegasus Books.

Jason, Lee-Roy and Wilbekin, Emil (2019), 'Botswana's metal subculture festival rocks', Afropunk, 1 July, https://afropunk.com/2019/07/botswanas-metal-subculture-festival-rocks/?fbclid=IwAR2N6wdZYcvihEbDu2hyqX6AzQOKCuLqOfNA9cvsTvqNBjlerPL1jBJNBvA. Accessed 1 July 2019.

Jay R 'Sleaze' (2018), e-mail to author, 23 January.

Jeong, Ho-Won (ed.) (1999), *Conflict Resolution: Dynamics, Process and Structure*, Aldershot: Ashgate.

Kabaka, Daudi (1965), 'Harambee, Harambee', *Harambee/Bibi Moupe,* 7", Kenya: Equator Records.

Kagwanja, Peter Mwangi (2005), 'Power to *Uhuru*': Youth identity and generational politics in Kenya's 2002 election', *African Affairs*, 105:418, pp. 51–75.

Kahn-Harris, Keith (2000), '"Roots"?: The relationship between the global and the local within the extreme metal scene', *Popular Music*, 19, pp. 13–30.

Kahn-Harris, Keith (2011a), 'Botswana's cowboy metalheads', *Vice*, 31 March, https://www.vice.com/en/article/3b5pp3/atlas-hoods-botswanas-cowboy-metalheads. Accessed 31 May 2019.

Kahn-Harris, Keith (2011b), 'You are from Israel and that is enough to hate you forever', in J. Wallach, H. M. Berger and P. D. Greene (eds), *Metal Rules the Globe: Heavy Metal Music Around the World*, Durham: Duke University Press, pp. 200–23.

Kahn-Harris, Keith (2013), *Extreme Metal: Music and Culture on the Edge*, Oxford: Berg Publishers.

Kalia, Ammar (2020), 'Duma: Duma review—extreme Kenyan metalheads bring doom to the dance floor, *The Guardian*, 31 July, https://www.theguardian.com/music/2020/jul/31/duma-duma-review-nyege-nyege-tapes. Accessed 20 November 2020.

Kankan Bizin (2019), in-person interview with E. Banchs, Lomé, Togo, 20 September.

Kankan Bizin (2020), Skype interview with E. Banchs, 30 August.

Karwath, Rob and Davidson, Jean (1987), 'Alsip teens may have followed eastern suicide's lead', *Chicago Tribune*, 14 March, https://www.chicagotribune.com/news/ct-xpm-1987-03-14-8701200407-story.html. Accessed 14 March 2018.

Kelly, Kim (2018), 'The Queens of Botswana', *Metal Hammer*, 306 (March), pp. 70–72.

Kemp, Karl (2015), 'The rise, fall, and resurrection of South Africa's anti-occult police unit', *Vice*, 14 April, https://www.vice.com/en/article/xd7qk4/satanic-panic-the-history-of-south-africas-specialised-anti-occult-police-unit-394. Accessed 13 March 2018.

Kemp, Simon (2020), 'Digital 2020: Global digital overview', DataReportal, https://datareportal.com/reports/digital-2020-global-digital-overview. Accessed 26 October 2020.

Kendi, Ibram X (2019), *How to be an Antiracist*, New York: One World.

Kiereini, Douglas (2018), 'Peter Colmore: The father of modern Kenyan advertising', *Business Daily*, 17 May, https://www.businessdailyafrica.com/bd/lifestyle/society/peter-colmore-the-father-of-modern-kenyan-advertising-2202734. Accessed 4 May 2019.

Killingray, David (2010), *Fighting for Britain: African Soldiers in the Second World War*, Woodbridge, Suffolk: James Currey.

King, Rudith S. and Amponsah, Owusu (2012), 'The role of city authorities in contributing to the development of urban slums in Ghana', *Journal of Construction Project Management and Innovation* 2:1, pp. 285–313.

Ki-Zerbo, Joseph, Mazrui, Ali A., Wondji, Christhope and Boahen Adu A. (1993), 'Nation-building and changing political values', in A. A. Mazrui and C. Wondji (eds), *UNESCO General History of Africa VIII: African Since 1935*, Paris, Oxford and Berkeley, CA: UNESCO, James Currey and University of California Press, pp. 468–98.

Klopper, Annie (2011), '"In ferocious anger I bite the hand that controls": The rise of Afrikaans punk rock music', in A. Grundlingh and S. Huigen (eds), *Reshaping Remembrance: Critical Essays on Afrikaans Places of Memory*, Amsterdam: Rosenberg Publishers, pp. 179–89.

Klypchak, Brad (2011), 'How you gonna see me know: Recontextualizing metal artists and moral panics', *Popular Music History*, 6:1/2, pp. 38–51.

Knopke, Eckhardt (2019), 'Heavy metal in Kenya', in D. Horn, J. Sheperd (eds), *Bloomsbury Encyclopedia of Popular Music of the World Volume XII*, New York: Bloomsbury Academic, pp. 188–90.

Kotarba, Joseph, A. and Vannini, Phillip (2009), *Understanding Society through Popular Music*, New York and London: Routledge.

Kraidy, Marwan, M. (2005), *Hybridity, or the Cultural Logic of Globalization*, Philadelphia: Temple University Press.

Kruse, Holly (1993), 'Subcultural identity in alternative music culture', *Popular Music*, 12:1, pp. 33–41.

Kumah-Abiwu, Felix (2016), 'Leadership traits and Ghana's foreign policy: The case of Jerry Rawling's foreign economic policy of the 1980s', *The Round Table*, 105:3, pp. 297–310.

Lach, Stef (2016), 'Rotting Christ to change name for South African gig', *Metal Hammer*, 10 March, https://www.loudersound.com/news/rotting-christ-to-change-name-for-south-africa-gigs. Accessed 9 August 2019.

Last Year's Tragedy (2011a), 'A Tribute to Anarchy', *A Tribute to Anarchy*, digital single, Kenya: Andromeda Music.

Last Year's Tragedy (2011b), 'A Tribute to Anarchy', Blogspot, 19 April, http://lastyearstragedy.blogspot.com/2011/04/tribute-to-anarchy.html. Accessed 1 September 2019.

Last Year's Tragedy (2013a), 'Challenge Accepted', *Challenge Accepted*, digital EP, Kenya: Andromeda Music.

Last Year's Tragedy (2013b), 'March from the Underground', *Challenge Accepted*, digital EP, Kenya: Andromeda Music.

Last Year's Tragedy (2020), 'Pounds for Flesh', *Amongst Lions*, digital LP, Kenya: Andromeda Music.

Lee, Dennis William (2018), '"Negeri Seribu Bangsa": Musical hybridization in contemporary Indonesian death metal', *Metal Music Studies*, 4:3, pp. 531–48.

Lelliott, Judy (2015), 'Who are the death metal cowboys of Africa?', *Seeker Stories*, 16 June, https://www.youtube.com/watch?v=076N6Xu8fGc. Accessed 6 June 2020.

Lennon, John (1971), 'Imagine', *Imagine*, LP, South Africa: Parlophone.

Levtzion, Nehemia (1963), 'The thirteenth and fourteenth century kings of Mali', *The Journal of African History*, 4:3, pp. 341–53.

Linkin Park (2000), *Hybrid Theory*, CD, USA: Warner Bros. Records.

Linkin Park (2008), *Road to Revolution: Live at Milton Keynes*, CD/DVD, USA: Warner Bros.

Little, Bryan (2009), *Fokofpolisiekar: Forgive Them for They Know Not What They Do*, South Africa: Journeyman Pictures.

Lodge, Tom (2013), 'Alternation and leadership succession in African democracies', *Irish Studies in International Affairs*, 24, pp. 21–40.

Low, John (1982), 'A history of Kenyan guitar music: 1945–80', *African Music*, 6:2 pp. 17–36.

Löwe, Philipp (2016), 'Heavy metal ist ihre religion', *Der Spiegel*, 8 November, https://www.spiegel.de/stil/heavy-metal-fotoprojekt-hellbangers-aus-botswana-a-1119030.html. Accessed 4 June 2019.

Lucey, Roger (1979), 'Lungile Tabalaza', *The Road is Much Longer*, LP, South Africa: 3rd Ear Music.

Lulat, Y. G. -M. (2008), *United States Relations with South Africa: A Critical Overview from the Colonial Period to the Present*, New York: Peter Lang Publishing, Inc.

Lull, James (2000), *Media, Communication, Culture: A Global Approach*, 2nd ed., New York: Columbia University Press.

Lynch, Gabrielle (2006), 'Negotiating ethnicity: Identity politics in contemporary Kenya', *Review of African Political Economy*, 33:107, pp. 49–65.

Mack, John (1994), 'African masking', in J. Mack (ed.), *Masks: The Art of Expression*, London: British Museum Press [published for the Trustees of the British Museum], pp. 32–55.

Madondo, Bongani (2017), 'Far beyond driven', *Huck*, 'The Outsider Issue', 60 (June/July), pp. 23–30.

Mahon, Maureen (2004), *Right to Rock: The Black Rock Coalition and the Cultural Politics of Race*, Durham: Duke University Press.

Mallon, Sean (2010), 'Against tradition', *The Contemporary Pacific*, 2:2, pp. 362–81.

Marcus, George E. (2006) 'Where have all the tales of fieldwork gone?', *Ethnos*, 71:1, pp. 113–22.

Marshall, Frank (2012), 'Visions of renegades', *Transition*, 109, pp. 63–71.

Marshall, Frank (2019), e-mail to author, 30 October.

Martens, Claire (2019), e-mail to author, 28 January.

Martin, Glen (1997), 'Youth sentenced in girl's horrific slaying:15-year-old "sacrificed" in satanic plot', *San Francisco Chronicle*, 8 March, https://www.sfgate.com/news/article/Youth-Sentenced-in-Girl-s-Horrific-Slaying-2852135.php. Accessed 6 May 2018.

Matiha, Dumisani 'Dumi'(2020), e-mail to author, 5 June.

Mayer, Adam and Timberlake, Jeffrey M. (2014), '"The fist in the face of god": Heavy metal music and decentralized cultural diffusion', *Sociological Perspectives*, 57:1, pp. 27–51.

Mazrui, Ali A. (1968), ''Thoughts on assassination in Africa', *Political Science Quarterly*, 83:1, pp. 44–58.

McDougal, Dennis (1986), 'Osbourne denounces suit in teenager's suicide', *LA Times*, 22 January, https://www.latimes.com/archives/la-xpm-1986-01-22-ca-31687-story.html. Accessed 6 May 2018.

McGrath, Bill (2015), 'The othering of Botswanan metal,' in T. M. Karjalainen and K. Kärki (eds), *Modern Heavy Metal: Markets, Practices and Cultures*, International Academic Research Conference, Helsinki, Finland, 8–12 June, Finland: Aalto University Publication Series, pp. 206-18.

McGroarty, Patrick (2016), 'Shout of Africa: Heavy metal maniacs swarm the Kalahari—Botswana is home to a raucous festival, starring Overthrust and a lot of leather', *Wall Street Journal*, 8 June, pp. A–1.

MDG Monitor (n.d.), 'Category: Millennium Development Goals', https://www.mdgmonitor.org/millennium-development-goals/. Accessed 24 September 2020.

Mechanic, Michael and Bonet, Pep (2017), 'These photos of Botswanan metalheads are pretty mind-blowing: In the middle of Africa's Kalahari desert, a thriving "Hellbanger scene"',

Mother Jones, January/February, https://www.motherjones.com/media/2017/02/heavy-metal-botswana-pep-bonet/. Accessed 29 May 2019.

Meredith, Martin (2005), *The Fate of Africa: From the Hopes of Freedom to the Heart of Despair: A History of 50 Years of Independence*, New York: Public Affairs.

Meredith, Martin (2007), *Diamonds, Gold and War: The British, the Boers and the Making of South Africa*, New York: Public Affairs.

Meredith, Martin (2014), *The Fortunes of Africa: A 5000-Year History of Wealth, Greed and Endeavor*, New York: Public Affairs.

Metal Orizon (1999), *Ancestral Blessing*, Botswana: Afro-Angel.

Metal Orizon (2001), 'We Are Rolling', *Myopic Enslavement*, Botswana: Afro-Angel.

Metal4Africa (2020), 'The line-up for SummerFest '21 includes', Facebook, 24 November, https://www.facebook.com/metal4africa/photos/a.10150589897021363/10157426507376363. Accessed 28 November 2020.

Metropolis (2013), 'Bunny hugging metal heads in Botswana', *Metropolis*, 31 January, https://www.youtube.com/watch?v=khOBsKum9DI. Accessed 6 June 2020.

Mgadla, P. T. (2014), 'Racial discrimination in colonial Botswana: 1946–65', *South African Historical Journal*, 66:3, pp. 486–503

Michaels, Sean (2008), 'Slipknot blamed for inspiring school murder', *The Guardian*, 21 August, https://www.theguardian.com/music/2008/aug/21/slipknot.school.killing. Accessed 6 May 2018.

Miller, George and Ogilvie, George (1985), *Mad Max Beyond Thunderdome*, USA: Warner Bros.

Mmonatau, Natasha (2014), 'Botswana's heavy metal cowboys photographed in Gaborone', *Okay Africa*, 12 November, https://www.okayafrica.com/botswana-heavy-metal-cowboys-ma-rock-aldo-brincat-photos/. Accessed 31 May 2019.

Monster Children (2019), 'Soweto is the future of punk', *Monster of Children*, 62, 19 April, https://www.monsterchildren.com/future-of-punk-soweto-karabo-mooki/. Accessed 19 August 2010.

Mooney, Katie (1998), '"Ducktails, flick-knives and pugnacity": Subcultural and hegemonic masculinities in South Africa, 1948–60', *Journal of Southern African Studies*, 24:4, Special Issue: 'Masculinities', pp.753–74.

Mosca, Raffaele (2014), *March of the Gods: Botswana Metalheads*, Italy: Self-released.

Motörhead (1980), *Ace of Spades*, LP, UK: Bronze Records.

Murphy, David (2007), 'Where does world music come from? Globalization, Afropop, and the question of cultural identity', in I. Biddle and V. Knights (eds), *Music, National Identity and the Politics of Location: Between the Global and the Local*, Aldershot: Ashgate Publishing, pp. 39–61.

Murphy, Kim (1986), 'Suit claiming ozzy osbourne led to suicide dismissed', *LA Times*, 20 December, https://www.latimes.com/archives/la-xpm-1986-12-20-mn-4460-story.html. Accessed 6 May 2018.

Mwangi, Daniel (2019), in-person interview with E. Banchs, Nairobi, Kenya, 30 September.

Mwendwa, Emmanuel (2019), 'Brief history overview of the Kenyan music scene', *Afro*, 7, https://afro7.net/brief-history-overview-of-the-kenyan-music-scene/. Accessed 29 May 2020.

Ndaba, Baldwin and Foss, Kanina (2009), 'I killed for attention, says teenager', *IOL*, 15 April, https://www.iol.co.za/news/south-africa/i-killed-for-attention-says-teenager-439992. Accessed 3 June 2018.

New York Times (1961), 'Togo backs Olympio', 11 April, https://timesmachine.nytimes.com/timesmachine/1961/04/11/118035363.html. Accessed 26 June 2020.

Nkrumah, Kwame (1964), *Consciencism: Philosophy and Ideology for De-Colonization*, New York: Monthly Review Press.

Nilsson, Magnus (2019), 'Heavy metal in Botswana', in D. Horn and J. Shepherd (eds), *Blooms-bury Encyclopedia of Popular Music of the World Vol XII, Genres: Sub-Saharan Africa*, New York: Bloomsbury Academic, pp. 185–88.

Nordström, Susanna and Herz, Marcus (2013), '"It's a matter of being eaten": Gender positioning and difference making in the heavy metal subculture', *European Journal of Cultural Studies*, 16:4, pp. 453–67.

Northey, Sashquita (2020), e-mail to author, 1 April.

Nosey Road (1983), *Freeway*, LP, South Africa: Gallo.

Nyairo, Joyce (2005), '*Zilizopwenda*: Kayamba Afrika's use of cover versions, remix, and sampling in the (re)membering of Kenya', *African Studies*, 64:1 (July), pp. 29–54.

Nyairo, Joyce and Ogude, James (2005), 'Popular music, popular politics: *Unbwogable* and the idioms of freedom in kenyan popular music', *African Affairs*, 104: 15 (April), pp. 225–49.

O'Boyle, Tom (2020), 'Kenyan noise kings Duma make industrial grindcore like you've never heard it before', 20 October, *Metal Hammer*, https://www.loudersound.com/features/kenyan-noise-kings-duma-make-industrial-grindcore-like-youve-never-heard-it-before?fbclid=IwAR3QGhljHV-JWSVwjh8Wiedu5Sx8Q1LEFF5ArfoBPXPIY25chS-oXHgzwXo. Accessed 20 November 2020.

Obeng-Odom, Franklin and Amedzro, Laurence (2011), 'Inadequate housing in Ghana', *Ubani izziv*, 22:1, pp. 127–37.

O'Connell, John M. (ed.) (2010), 'An ethnomusicological approach to music and conflict', *Music and Conflict*, Champaign, Illinois: University of Illinois Press.

Odidi, Bill (2013a), 'The golden years of kenya's music,' *Daily Nation*, 12 August, https://www.nation.co.ke/lifestyle/dn2/The-golden-years-of-Kenyas-music/957860–1944042-ml-2jdk/index.html. Accessed 4 May 2020.

Odidi, Bill (2013b), 'US, British origin of "Harambee" melody', *Daily Nation*, 28 July, https://nation.africa/kenya/life-and-style/dn2/us-british-origin-of-harambee-melo-dy--878892?view=htmlamp. Accessed 4 May 2020.

Odidi, Bill (2019), in-person interview with E. Banchs, Nairobi, Kenya, 1 October.

O'Flynn, John (2007), 'National identity and music in transition: Issues of authenticity in a global setting', in I. Biddle and V. Knights (eds), *Music, National Identity and the Politics of Location: Between the Global and the Local*, Aldershot: Ashgate Publishing, pp. 19–38.

Ojiro, Willy (2019), e-mail to author, 25 November.

Okoli, Chika (2017), 'Botswana's metal heads—The Marockos', *OkayAfrica*, 20 September, https://www.youtube.com/watch?v=6Ir3OyIBR0Y. Accessed 6 June 2020.

O'Malley, Mark (2010), 'Ewe', in K. Anthony Appiah and H. L. Gates Jr. (eds), *Encyclopedia of Africa*, vol. 1, Oxford: Oxford University Press, pp. 454–55.

Omond, Roger (1985), *The Apartheid Handbook: A Guide to South Africa's Everyday Racial Policies*, New York: Penguin Press.

Osibisa (1971), 'Music For Gong Gong', *Music For Gong Gong*, 7" single, UK: MCA Records.

Owusu , George, Agyei-Mensah, Samuel and Ragnhild, Lund (2008), 'Slums of hope and slums of despair: Mobility and livelihoods in Nima, Accra', *Norsk Geografisk Tidsskrift Norwegian Journal of Geography*, 62, pp. 180–90.

Oteng-Ababio, Martin and Grant, Richard (2020), 'E-waste recycling slum in the heart of Accra, Ghana: The dirty secrets', in M. Narasimha Vara Prasad, M. Vithanage and A. Borthakur (eds), *Handbook of Electronic Waste Management: International Best Practices and Case Studies*, Cambridge, MA and London: Butterworth-Heinemann, pp. 355–76.

Overell, Rosemary (2011), '"[I] hate girls and emo[tions]": Negotiating masculinity in grind-core music', *Popular Music History*, 6.1&2, pp. 198–223.

Owusu, George (2013), 'Coping with urban sprawl: A critical discussion of the urban containment strategy in a developing country city, Accra', *Planum: The Journal of Urbanism*, 26:1, pp. 1–17.

Palmer, Tony (1973), *Ginger Baker in Africa*, UK: Eagle Vision.

Pasbani, Robert (2015), 'South African metal fest forced to change venue three times due to religious backlash', *Metal Injection*, 16 January, https://metalinjection.net/news/south-african-metal-fest-forced-to-change-venues-three-times-due-to-religious-backlash. Accessed 9 August 2019.

Patterson, D. (1999), 'The life and times of Kenyan pop', in S. Broughton, M. Ellingham and R. Trillo (eds), *World Music: The Rough Guide*, vol. 1, London: Penguin, pp. 509–22.

Pearson, Clive (2020), Skype interview with E. Banchs, 16 February.

Philips, Chuck (1990), 'Another day in court for rock music: Law: Just weeks after the Judas Priest case, Ozzy Osbourne faces similar suits over subliminal', *LA Times*, 4 October, https://www.latimes.com/archives/la-xpm-1990-10-04-ca-2501-story.html. Accessed 6 May 2018.

Phillipov, Michelle (2012), 'Extreme music for extreme people?: Norwegian black metal and transcendent violence', *Popular Music History*, 6.1&2, pp. 150–63.

Picton, John (1990), 'What's in a mask', *African Languages and Cultures*, 3:2, pp. 181–202.

Pindral, Bianca (2018), 'Today, 10 years ago, a boy walked into his school with a Samuri sword …' *Krugersdorp News*, 17 August, https://planetafropunk.com/?ga=2.136991856.1551253116.1606240918-974783693.1606240918. Accessed 15 August 2019.

Pink Floyd (1979) 'Another brick in the wall', *The Wall*, 2XLP, South Africa: CBS.

Planet Afropunk (2020), 'Live streaming event', *Afropunk*, 23–25 October, https://planetafropunk.com/?ga=2.136991856.1551253116.1606240918-974783693.1606240918. Accessed 23 October 2020.

Plessis, Leané du and Roestoff, Amanda (2008), 'Want to see something cool?', *News 24*, 18 August, https://www.news24.com/news24/want-to-see-something-cool-20080818. Accessed 15 August 2019.

Powerslide (2019), 'Banana republic', *Cheshire Grin*, digital LP, Kenya: Bin Khalid Sonic Pollution.

Pyykkönen, Samuli (2018), *Freedom in the Dark: A Roadtrip to Trans-Kalahari Rock 'N' Roll*, Finland: Self-released.

Rabbitt (1976), 'Charlie', *Charlie/Looking for the Man*, LP, South Africa: JoBurg Records.

Ranger, Terrance (1992), 'The invention of tradition in colonial Africa', in E. Hobsbawm and T. Ranger (eds), *The Invention of Tradition*, Cambridge: Cambridge University Press, pp. 211–62.

Reitov, Ole (2004), 'Encounters with a South African censor: Confrontation and reconciliation', in M. Korpe (ed.), *Shoot the Singer!: Music Censorship Today*, London: Zed Books, pp. 82–93.

Reporters Without Borders (RSF) (2019), 'World press freedom index 2019', https://rsf.org/en/togo. Accessed 25 November 2019.

Reyes-Kulkarni, Saby (2016), 'Greetings from the third world: Revisiting Sepultura's genre-changing "Roots"', *Pop Matters*, 29 March, https://www.popmatters.com/greetings-from-the-third-world-revisiting-sepulturas-genre-changing-roots-2495442037.html?rebelltitem=1#rebelltitem1. Accessed 10 October 2019.

Richards, Paul (1995), 'Rebellion in Liberia and Sierra Leone: A crisis of youth?', in O. W. Furley (ed.), *Conflict in Africa*, London: I.B. Tauris, pp. 134–70.

Riches, Gabby (2015), 'Re-conceptualizing women's marginalization in heavy metal: A feminist post-structuralist perspective', *Metal Music Studies*, 1:2, pp. 263–70.

Riches, Gabrielle (2011), 'Embracing the chaos: Most pits, extreme metal music and liminality', *Journal for Cultural Research*, 15:3, pp. 315–32.

Ritter, Andrea Von (2017), 'Die Wüste Bedt!: Ein paar Büsche und Bäume, viel Sand und wenig los: Dast ist der kleine Ort Ghanzi in Botsuana: Einmal im Jahr aber dröhnen hier Gitarren und röhren heisere Stimmen—beim einzigen Heavy Metal Festival in der Savanne Afrikas', *Die Stern*, 6 July, pp. 74–84.

Robertson, Mary (2011), 'The constraints of colour: Popular music listening and the interrogation of "race" in post-apartheid South Africa', *popular Music*, 30:3, pp. 455–70.

Rock (2019), in-person interview with E. Banchs, Lomé, Togo, 22 September.

Rodriguez, Jason (2006), 'Color-blind ideology and the cultural appropriation of hip-hop', *Journal of Contemporary Ethnography*, 35:6, pp.645–68.

Rogers, Richard A. (2006), 'From cultural exchange to transculturation: A review and reconceptualization of cultural appropriation', *Communication Theory*, 16, pp. 474–503.

Rolinec, Petra (2019), e-mail to author, 19 October.

Rotberg, Robert (1965), *A Political History of Tropical Africa*, New York: Harcourt, Brace & World, Inc.

Roux, Kabous le (2017), 'On this day in 1976 South Africa became one of the last countries to get TV', *Cape Talk*, 5 January, http://www.capetalk.co.za/articles/238124/sabc-tv-turns-40. Accessed 6 June 2017.

Rowe, Paula (2018), *Heavy Metal Youth Identities: Researching the Musical Empowerment of Youth Transitions and Psychosocial Wellbeing*, Bingley: Emerald Press.

Saibore, Brian (2019), in-person interview with E. Banchs, Nairobi, Kenya, 2 October.

Saibou, Marceline (2016), *Presence, Absence and Disjunctures: Popular Music and Politics in Lomé, Togo, 1967–2005*, Ph.D thesis, New York: Columbia University.

Said, Edward (1993), *Culture and Imperialism*, London: Chatto & Windus.

Said, Edward (1994), *Orientalism: 25th Anniversary Edition*, New York: Vintage Books.

Sajnani, Damon (2013), 'Troubling the trope of "Rapper as Modern Griot"', *The Journal of Pan-African Studies*, 6:3, pp. 156–80.

Sale, Kirk J. (1965), 'The loneliness of Kwame Nkrumah', *The New York Times Magazine*, 27 June, pp. 20–21 and 38–43, https://timesmachine.nytimes.com/timesmachine/1965/06/27/issue.html. Accessed 12 August 2020.

Salm, Steven J. and Falola, Toyin (2002), *Culture and Customs of Ghana*, Westport, CT: Greenwood Press.

Sanders, Denis (1971), *Soul to Soul*, USA: Cinerama Releasing Corporation.

Sarr, Felwine (2019), *Afrotopia* (trans. D. S. Burke and S. Jones-Boardman), Minneapolis: University of Minnesota Press.

Sbrana, Giuseppe (2020), e-mail to author, 3 June.

Schaap, Julian (2019), 'Elvis has finally left the building? Boundary work, whiteness and the reception of rock music in comparative perspective', Ph.D. thesis, Rotterdam: Erasmus University.

Schaap, Julian and Berkers, Pauwke (2020), 'Your're not supposed to be into rock music: Authenticity maneuvering in a white configuration', *Sociology of Race and Ethnicity*, pp. 1–15.

Scherzinger, Martin (2004), '"Art" music in a cross-cultural context: The case of Africa', in N. Cook and A. Pople (eds), *The Cambridge History of Twentieth-Century Music*, Cambridge: Cambridge UniversityPress, pp. 584–614.

Schoonraad, Robert (2020), Skype interview with E. Banchs, 1 February.

Schumann, Anne (2008), 'The beat that beat apartheid: The role of music in the resistance against apartheid in South Africa', *Stichproben: Wiener Zeitschrift für kritische Afrikastudien*, 14:8, pp. 17–39.

Seal, Rodney (1988), *Rock Musiek: Die reg om te weet*, 2nd ed., South Africa: M.F.Y.

Sears, Fred F. (1956), *Rock Around the Clock*, USA: Columbia Pictures.

Segy, Ladislas (1976), *Masks of Black Africa*, USA: Dover Publications.

Sepultura (1996), *Roots*, CD, USA: Roadrunner Records.

Shepler, Susan (2010), 'Youth music and politics in post-war Sierra Leone', *The Journal of Modern African Studies*, 48:4, pp. 627–42.

Shiakallis, Paul (2015a), 'The leather-clad rock queens of Botswana—in pictures', *The Guardian*, 25 December, https://www.theguardian.com/world/gallery/2015/dec/25/the-leather-clad-rock-queens-of-botswana-in-pictures. Accessed 18 July 2019.

Shiakallis, Paul (2015b), *Leathered Skins, Unchained Hearts*, Paul Shiakallis Official Website, paulshiakallis.com http://www.paulshiakallis.com/2594099-leathered-skins-unchained-hearts. Accessed 31 May 2019.

Shiakallis, Paul (2019), e-mail to author, 1 November.

Shoup, John (1997), 'Pop music and resistance in apartheid South Africa', *Alif: Journal of Comparative Poetics*, 17, pp. 73–92.

Skinflint (2018), *Skinflint*, CD, UK: Into Records.

Smith, Dean (2020), e-mail to author, 21 February.

South African Government Census (2011), 'Home page', www.statssa.gov.za. Accessed 2 October 2018.

South African Rock Encyclopedia (2020), 'Home page', http://rock.co.za. Accessed 4 November 2020.

Staszak, Jean-Francois (2008), 'Other/otherness', *International Encyclopedia of Human Geography*, p.1–7.

Stokes, Martin (2008), 'On musical cosmopolitanism', *Macalester International*, 21:8, pp. 3–26.

Suburu, Ishmael Nommo (2018), 'List of some NGOs in Ghana', The Social Worker, 12 April, https://advocate200.wordpress.com/2018/04/12/list-of-some-ngos-in-ghana/. Accessed 3 September 2020.

Switch (2019), e-mail to author, 20 March.

Tamagni, Daniel (2013), 'Afrometals', *Daniel Tamagni Official Website*, http://www.danielet-amagni.com/afrometals/. Accessed 31 May 2019.

Tang, Patricia (2012), 'The rapper as modern griot: Reclaiming ancient traditions', in E. Charry (ed.), *Hip Hop Africa: New African Music in a Globalizing World*, Bloomington, IN: Indiana University Press, pp. 79–91.

Tepedelen, Adam (2018), 'Metal gods: The making of judas priest's *Stained Class*', *Decibel*, June, 164, pp. 55–64.

Teppo, Annika (2009), 'My mouse is protected by a dragon: White South Africans, magic and sacred spaces in post-apartheid cape town', *Suomen Anthropologi: Journal of the Finnish Anthropological Society*, 34:1, pp. 19–41.

The News (1981), 'Up to No Good'/'Station Road Rhythm', *Up to No Good/Station Road Rhythm*, single, South Africa: Mountain Records.

The Tribune Staff ([1995] 2012), 'Elyse Pahler: Killed in Nipomo in 1995', *The Tribune*, [14 April] 26 June, https://www.sanluisobispo.com/news/local/crime/article39122823.html. Accessed 6 June 2017.

Todisco, Arianna (2020), 'Community hall', Arianna Todisco Official Website, https://www.ariannatodisco.it/communityhall-p20893. Accessed 24 January 2020.

Trupp, Alexander (2011), 'Exhibiting the "other" then and now: "Human zoos" in Southern China and Thailand', *ASEAS – Austrian Journal of South-East Asian Studies*, 4:1, pp. 139–49.

Tunstall, Jeremy (1977), *The Media are American*, Beverly Hills, CA and London: Sage/ Constable.

UN-Habitat (2019), *Strategic Plan 2020-2023*, https://unhabitat.org/sites/default/files/documents/2019-09/strategic_plan_2020-2023.pdf. Accessed 25 September 2020.

UN-Stats (2018), 'Sustainable cities and communities', https://unstats.un.org/sdgs/report/2019/ goal-11/. Accessed 24 September 2020.

Varas-Díaz, Nelson (2021), *Decolonial Metal Music in Latin America*, Bristol, UK: Intellect.

Varas-Díaz, Nelson, Mendoza, Sigrid, Rivera-Segarra, Eliut and González-Sepúlveda, Osvaldo (2016), 'Methodological strategies and challenges in research with small heavy metal scenes: A reflection on entrance, evolution and permanence', *Metal Music Studies*, 2:3, pp. 273–90.

Varas-Díaz, Nelson, Rivera-Segarra, Eliut and Nevárez, Daniel (2019), 'Coloniality and resistance in Latin American metal music: Death as experience and strategy', in D. Castillo and B. Nelson (eds), *Writing in the End Times: Apocalyptic Imagination in the Hispanic World: Hispanic Issues On Line*, 23, pp. 226–51.

Varas-Díaz, Nelson, Rivera-Segarra, Eliut, Rivera Medina, C. L., Mendoza, Sigrid and Gonzalez-Sepulveda, Osvaldo (2015), 'Predictors of communal formation in a small heavy metal scene: Puerto Rico as a case study', *Metal Music Studies*, 1:1, pp. 87–103.

Vas, Marq (2020), Skype interview with E. Banchs, 2 March.

Vasan, Sonia (2011), 'The price of rebellion: Gender boundaries in the death metal scene', *Journal for Cultural Research*, 15:3, pp. 333–49.

Verini, James (2016), 'The Prosecutor and the President', *The New York Times Magazine*, 26 June, https://www.nytimes.com/2016/06/26/magazine/international-criminal-court-moreno-ocampo-the-prosecutor-and-the-president.html?searchResultPosition=5. Accessed 26 October 2020.

Vianney, Sarah (2019) *Queens of Botswana*, UK: 1091 Media.

Victor, Jeffrey S. (1993), *Satanic Panic: The Creation of a Contemporary Legend*, Chicago: Open Court.

Vulture (2020), e-mail to author, 5 June.

Wakesa, Peter W. (2004), 'The politics of marginal forms: Popular music, cultural identity and political opposition in Kenya', *Africa Development*, 29:4, pp. 92–112.

Walker, Gary (2020), e-mail to author, 28 January.

Wallace, Aminah (2014), 'Pan-Africanism and slave rebellions,' in T. Falola and K. Essien (eds), *Pan Africanism, and the Politics of African Citizenship and Identity*, New York and London: Routledge, pp. 59-84.

Wallach, Jeremy, Berger, Harris M. and Greene, Paul D. (eds) (2011), *Metal Rules the Globe: Heavy Metal Music Around the Globe*, Durham: Duke University Press.

Walser, Robert (2004), 'Forging masculinity: Heavy metal sounds and images of gender', in S. Frith (ed.), *Popular Music: Critical Concepts in Media and Cultural Studies, Volume II: The Rock Era*, London and New York: Routledge, pp. 343–72.

Wanyama, Mellitus Nyongesa (2019), 'Litungu music', in D. Horn, David, J. Shepard (eds), *Bloomsbury Encyclopedia of Popular Music of the World Vol. XII*, New York: Bloomsbury Academic, pp. 362–65.

Waters, Roger (2011), 'Tear down this Israeli wall opinion', *The Guardian*, 11 March, https://www.theguardian.com/commentisfree/2011/mar/11/cultural-boycott-west-bank-wall. Accessed 13 August 2019.

Wehelie, Benazir (2016), 'Heavy metal finds a home in Botswana', *CNN Style*, 30 August, https://www.cnn.com/style/article/cnnphotos-heavy-metal-botswana/index.html. Accessed 29 May 2019.

Weinstein, Deena (2000) *Heavy Metal: The Music and Its Culture*, New York: De Capo.

Weinstein, Deena (2016), 'Communities of metal: Ideal, diminished and imaginary', in N. Varas-Díaz and N. Scott (eds), *Heavy Metal Music and the Communal Experience*, Lanham: Lexington Books, pp. 3–22.

Wendt, Albert (1976), 'Towards a new Oceania', *Mana Review*, 1:1, pp. 49–60.

Wiederhorn, Jon (2017), 'Max Cavalera on Sepultura's "Really Strange", Groundbreaking album "Chaos A.D"', *Revolver*, 19 October, https://www.revolvermag.com/music/max-cavalera-sepul-turas-really-strange-groundbreaking-album-chaos-ad. Accessed 26 November 2019.

Williams, Duncan and Da Rocha, Marcio Alves (2017), 'Decoding cultural signifiers of Brazil-ian identity and the African diaspora from the music of Sepultura', *Metal Music Studies*, 3:1, pp. 145–52.

Williams, Fahidi (1960), *Malaika*, LP, Kenya: EMI.

World Bank (2019a), 'Data: Togo', 18 October, https://data.worldbank.org/country/togo. Accessed 10 November 2020.

World Bank (2019b), 'Gross domestic product 2019', https://databank.worldbank.org/data/download/GDP.pdf. Accessed 25 September 2020.

World Bank (2020), 'COVID-19 to add as many as 150 Million extreme poor by 2021', 7 October, https://www.worldbank.org/en/news/press-release/2020/10/07/covid-19-to-add-as-many-as-150-million-extreme-poor-by-2021. Accessed 24 November 2020.

World Health Organization (2020), 'WHO coronavirus disease (COVID-19) dashboard', 28 November, https://covid19.who.int. Accessed 28 November 2020.

World Inequality Database (WID) (2020), https://wid.world/country/kenya/. Accessed 23 September 2020.

World Population Review (2020), 'Accra population 2020', https://worldpopulationreview.com/world-cities/accra-population. Accessed 25 September 2020.

Wright, George (2019), 'Doch Chkae, the metal band born on a rubbish dump', BBC, 6 October, https://www.bbc.co.uk/news/world-asia-49795218. Accessed 21 September 2020.

Wrust (2007), *Soulless Machine*, CD, Botswana: Witchdoctor.

Xenostate (2013), in-person interview, Nairobi, Kenya, 18 October.

Yeboah, Thomas, Owusu, Lucy, Arhin, Albert A. and Kumi, Emmanuel (2015), 'Fighting poverty from the street: Perspectives of some female informal sector workers on gendered poverty and livelihood portfolios in Southern Ghana', *Journal of Economic and Social Studies*, 5:1, pp. 239–67.

Yeebo, Yepoka (2014), 'Inside a massive electronics graveyard', *The Atlantic*, 29 December, https://www.theatlantic.com/technology/archive/2014/12/inside-a-massive-electronics-graveyard/383922/. Accessed 28 August 2020.

Ziff, Bruce and Rao, Pratima V. (1997), 'Introduction to cultural appropriation: A framework for analysis', in B. Ziff and P. V. Rao (eds), *Borrowed Power: Essays On Cultural Appropriation*, New Brunswick, NJ: Rutgers University Press, pp. 1–27.

Index

Printed in the USA
CPSIA information can be obtained
at www.ICGtesting.com
LVHW081228060824
787441LV00001B/4